A Faulty Foundation

A FAULTY FOUNDATION

How Lordship Salvation Negatively Impacts the Christian Life

John Thomas Clark, Thm, DMin
Tetelestai Press

A Faulty Foundation: How Lordship Salvation Negatively Impacts the Christian Life
© 2021 Copyright by John Thomas Clark
Published by Tetelestai Press

ISBN: 978-1-7353359-4-0

TABLE OF CONTENTS

INTRODUCTION

I still remember how angry I was when I was first exposed to "gospel clarity" teaching. A dear friend of mine (Robert Ambs) had shared an audio cassette tape of this teaching from Pastor Dennis Rokser in Duluth, Minnesota. I was irritated! This pastor was basically saying that what I believed was wrong, what I taught was wrong, and the way I was doing evangelism was wrong. About 30 minutes in to the tape, I ejected it, set it on my dash, and began thinking of a way that I could tell my friend Robert that I had listened to it, even though I really did not finish it.

However, two weeks passed, and I could never quite get comfortable lying to my friend, so I popped the tape back in to finish it. With the Lord's continual softening of my heart to the truth, I was at last ready to receive the clarity teaching with an open heart. That was September of 2000. I was a newly married high school math teacher who was very active as a layperson in my local church. I remember how excited I was! I remember thinking, "Everyone needs to hear this message of clarity! Everyone needs to focus solely on the finished work of Jesus Christ! Everyone is going to love hearing about this!"

The church I was attending at the time was not convinced. In fact, they felt I had gone off the deep end, concerning myself too much with "semantics," as they would call it. It did not matter to them if you said, "Give your life to Christ, ask Jesus into your heart, pray the sinner's prayer, commit your life to Christ, surrender your all to Christ, make Christ the Lord of your life, walk the aisle, ask for forgiveness, or believe on the Lord Jesus Christ." All of these, in their thinking, were saying the same thing and basically meant the same thing. It was this initial opposition that created in me a passion to dig deeper and to understand more fully the gospel I was proclaiming.

Additionally, it was in this local church that some men convinced me that my dad, who was in the process of divorcing my mom, was not really saved since he was living carnally and had not submitted to the Lordship of Christ. I spent years every Sunday night with a group of men in the church praying for all the "unsaved" dads in our body, including my dad. However, on a cool night in Portland, Oregon, in the summer of 1997, I spoke to my dad and asked him what his understanding of salvation was, and how he thought people got saved. He responded with a clear understanding of how Jesus Christ died (personally) for his sins and rose again, and he said he had put his faith in Christ alone in 1976. I was elated to hear my Dad express clear faith in Jesus Christ, but there was also great confusion. Why had the church been praying for his salvation all these years? Why did people in the church think he was unsaved? Was it because he had divorced his wife? Was it because he did not behave according to their understanding of true Christian values?

This was just the beginning of my negative exposure to the Lordship gospel. Over the years, I have seen countless people's lives destroyed by this teaching because the focus of this message is not on Jesus Christ and His finished work but rather on ourselves and our unfinished works. My heart's desire for this book is that each reader gains an even greater appreciation for the finished work of Jesus Christ! One word sums it up well – Τετέλεσται! (John 19:30)

DEDICATION

First and foremost, I give God all the praise and glory for His faithfulness in exposing me to sound Bible teaching in my life. Each day, I rejoice in the finished work of Jesus Christ more, and I am thankful for the men who have taught me clearly about the wonderful work of my Savior.

I am grateful to my wife, Carrie, who has supported me in many different ways. These include and are not limited to: (1) Supporting my desire to further my theological training at Tyndale Seminary and then Dallas Theological Seminary, (2) Functioning as my unofficial "grammar policewoman" throughout the writing process, and (3) Providing her unending love, support, and encouragement! Thanks, Honey!

I am so thankful for my kids (Abby, Cody, Riley, Sadie, and Tobin) who are also a huge blessing and motivation for me. I love you, kids, and pray God burns a clear gospel in your heart and a desire to share it with others. I pray that each and every day of your life that you see the value of what Jesus did for you!

My parents, Larry and Kathy Clark, who raised me in a Christian home and shared the gospel with me at five-years-old. I am eternally grateful to you both! My Dad passed away in 2019 from Alzheimer's Dementia, but he was truly one of the best friends I ever had. My Mom is still my number one fan (or #2 next to my wife) even after all the grief I put her through as a teenager! 😊

Bret Nazworth, a dear friend and mentor, who has invested his life in me. His influence is the primary reason I have a heart and passion for gospel clarity. He has taught me more than I probably know to give him credit for. He is a true disciple-maker of other disciple-makers. Love you, Bro!

Duluth Bible Church and Pastor Dennis Rokser, who through his audio teaching ministry, reinforced and clarified many different areas of Biblical doctrine for me. As a church, they have also invested time and resources in my ministry over the years through training and personal investment.

A special thanks to Emily Miller, a friend, and my administrative assistant, who made this project a reality with her work in putting together this Master's Thesis (originally) into book form.

A special thanks to my brother, Rick Clark, who designed the cover for me and designed the logo for Tetelestai Press.

Another special thanks to the following men who agreed to read through and provide critique of the manuscript at different stages along the way: Robert Ambs, Cody Hughes, Jeremy Jackson, Brad Maston, and Rob Armstrong.

Also, a special thanks to my current leadership board at Grace Community Fellowship in Newnan, Georgia. These men are huge supporters of any project or idea to further get the gospel out! I so appreciate working with them!

Additionally, I want to acknowledge a few others who have influenced me greatly and encouraged me with their words and their lives: Robert Ambs, Brad Smith, Ken Draper, and Rob Armstrong. I appreciate you all!

CHAPTER 1
What is Lordship Salvation?

In 1988, a storm hit the highlands of the Christian community. The storm itself had been brewing for a few decades prior to this time, yet it reached its climax in 1988. In an effort to clarify the gospel message, John F. MacArthur, Jr. wrote a book titled *The Gospel According to Jesus*, which didn't actually clarify the gospel but, rather, ignited a passionate debate that has continued to this day. The debate centers on the proper Biblical response to the gospel — in other words, what is required of and needed for somebody to become a Christian? The gospel response that MacArthur championed in his book has since become known as "lordship salvation."

In an effort to combat a shallow conversion and/or the scores of *Christians* (so called) who did not desire to live holy and righteous lives, lordship salvation was born. Although MacArthur was not the first person to champion this position, his goal of "clarifying the gospel" has become the most important and constant emphasis of his writing.[1] The lordship gospel attempts to curb any "light" consideration of salvific truths and puts a huge emphasis on the "seeker," who should count all costs of salvation before "jumping into it."

Charles C. Bing rightly states in his book, *Lordship Salvation: A Biblical Examination and Response*, "The designation 'Lordship Salvation' is reluctantly accepted by both proponents and opponents...as defined by its own advocates, Lordship Salvation could more properly be called 'Commitment Salvation,' 'Surrender Salvation,' or 'Submission Salvation.'"[2] In addition to simple faith in the person and work of Christ on the cross, the lordship camp teaches that one needs to submit or yield to Christ's lordship. In fact, they would include submission as a vital part of "saving faith." MacArthur states, "Yielding completely to Christ's lordship is that *vital* an element of true saving faith, and therefore, the proclamation of His lordship is an absolutely necessary component of the true gospel" (italics added).[3] If this were not clear

---

[1] John MacArthur, <u>Slave</u> (Nashville, TN.: Thomas Nelson, 2010), 1.

[2] Charles C. Bing, <u>Lordship Salvation: A Biblical Evaluation and Response. Grace Life Edition</u> (Burleson, TX: Grace Life Ministries, 1991), 5.

[3] John MacArthur, Jr., <u>The Gospel According to Jesus</u> (Grand Rapids: Zondervan, 1988), 36.

enough, elsewhere he states emphatically, "In fact, surrender to Christ is an important aspect of divinely produced saving faith, not something added to faith."[4]

For most believers, the discussion of Christ's lordship is a joyful one. The thought of having the One who died for the sins of the world, and who rose again, conquering death, as the Master and Lord of their lives is an exciting reality. In fact, the Bible tells us in Philippians 2:11 that, "...every tongue should confess that Jesus Christ *is* Lord, to the glory of God the Father." So not only will believers confess that Jesus Christ is Lord, but **everyone** will confess that He is Lord. Logically then, the lordship salvation issue is not whether or not Jesus is Lord or whether or not He is recognized as Lord because everyone is in agreement with this (or will be on some future date in eternity). As Dr. Charles Ryrie, free grace[5] proponent, a retired Professor of Systematic Theology at Dallas Theological Seminary, and author of the study notes for the *Ryrie Study Bible,* states, "Of course Jesus is Lord. He is Lord because of who He is. He is also Lord of creation, Lord of history, Lord of salvation, Lord of the church, Lord of disciples, Lord of the future. But even if there were no creation, no history, no salvation, no church, no disciples, no future, He was, is, and always will be Lord."[6] Thus, the issue is not *if* Jesus is Lord but rather the issue is **when**? When does the recognition or submission to the Lordship of Christ need to take place in regard to the issue of salvation? Is it even a component that even needs to be included in the gospel message?

The Greek word translated "Lord" is κύριος (*kurios)*, meaning "Lord, master, owner." In addition to references to the Lord Jesus, the word is used to refer to a possessor, owner, or master of property, households, servants, slaves. To add further weight to the meaning of this word, the word

---

[4] MacArthur, The Gospel According to Jesus, 43.

[5] The term "free grace" is a phrase commonly used to describe those who hold that for a person to go to heaven he or she must simply put his or her faith in Jesus Christ and His finished work alone. It is truly "grace alone through faith alone in Christ alone" with nothing added or subtracted. However, because of those promoting a "cross-less" gospel in our day (see The Gospel of the Christ by Dr. Tom Stegall for an excellent treatment of this topic), a more biblical terminology might be "true grace" as Peter describes in 1 Peter 5:12.

[6] Charles Ryrie, So Great Salvation: What It Means to Believe in Jesus Christ, (Wheaton, IL: Victor Books, 1989), 70.

κύριος (*kurios*) is used to translate the Hebrew word יהוה(*Yahweh*) in the Septuagint (LXX) over 8,600 times. It is used in the Shema found in Deuteronomy 6:4, "Hear, O Israel: The Lord (Yahweh/Kurios) our God, the Lord (Yahweh/Kurios) is one!" יהוה *(Yahweh)* was the official word used to describe the covenant-keeping God of Israel in the Old Testament and, therefore, has a very strong connection and implication regarding the deity of Jesus Christ. This is the way Paul uses the term κύριος (*kurios*) in Romans 10:9, "That if you confess with your mouth the Lord Jesus and believe in your heart that God has raised Him from the dead, you will be saved." The word translated "confess" is the Greek compound word ὁμολογέω (*homologeo*), meaning to say the same thing, to assent, to consent, to admit, or to agree with.[7] Notice in these passages, this is NOT a confession of sin or a feeling sorry for sin. On the contrary, this confession has nothing to do with sin and has everything to do with the identity of Jesus Christ. By using this word κύριος (*kurios)*, Paul is making a strong statement of Jesus' deity (i.e., His true identity). Paul's primary audience is a Jewish audience in this section of Romans, and he is telling them that they need to agree with God (and Paul) that Jesus Christ was indeed God and thus qualified to save them from their sins. In fact, if agree with God on Jesus' identity, then, when they called on the Lord (i.e., *Kurios*), they would be calling on Jesus Christ who could indeed save them (Romans 10:13). If they were unwilling to call upon Jesus Christ as Lord, they cannot be saved.

It is in this objective sense of the word "Lord" that the non-lordship position requires that unbelievers recognize the Lordship (i.e., deity) of Jesus Christ when they believe. "Confessing Jesus as Lord (God)" has nothing to do with what we do (i.e., surrendering our lives to Him, committing our all to Him), but it has everything to do with who Jesus is. It verifies *who* Jesus is, and it validates *what* Jesus did on the cross. In fact, Paul usually includes both the person (who Jesus is) and the work (death and resurrection) in his

---

[7] Spiros Zodhiates, The Complete Word Study Dictionary: New Testament, (Chattanooga, TN: AMG Publishers, 1992), 3670.

messages to unbelievers, as shown on his evangelistic missionary journeys.[8] This was the gospel that Paul preached.[9]

The disagreement comes when the lordship camp requires that unbelievers not only recognize Jesus Christ as Lord (deity) but also submit to His active reigning in their lives as a condition for salvation. The proof of this submission is then shown to be genuine through the believer's holy life — a life of minimal sin. As MacArthur states, "Salvation is by grace through faith. It has nothing to do with meritorious human works. But the only possible response to God's grace is a broken humility that causes the sinner to turn from his old life to Christ. The evidence of such a turning is the willingness to submit and obey. If coldhearted disobedience and deliberate rebellion continue unabated, there is good reason to doubt the reality of a person's faith."[10] MacArthur goes on to state, "He is Lord, and those who refuse Him as Lord cannot use Him as Savior. Everyone who receives Him must surrender to His authority, for to say we receive Christ when in fact we reject His right to reign over us is utter absurdity."[11]

To further illustrate this concept that unbelievers must submit to Jesus' active reigning in their lives to be assured of their salvation, we'll look at two additional lordship teachers. First, there is John Piper, who was the Pastor of Preaching and Vision at Bethlehem Baptist Church in Minneapolis, Minnesota from 1980-2013. Piper makes a statement in his book, *Future Grace*, that says, "But that does not mean that God does not produce in those 'justified' people (before and after the cross) an experiential righteousness that is not 'filthy rags.' In fact, he does; and this righteousness is precious to God and is required, not as the **ground** of our justification (which is the righteousness of Christ only), but as an **evidence** of our being truly justified children of God."[12] Another member of the lordship group is R.C. Sproul (1939-2017), who was the former Chairman of the Board of Ligonier Ministries, Professor of Systematic Theology at Reformed Theological Seminary, and Director

---

[8] "For I determined not to know anything among you except ***Jesus Christ*** and ***Him crucified***, (emphasis mine)," (1 Corinthians 2:2).

[9] "For I delivered to you first of all that which I also received: that Christ died for our sins according to the Scriptures, and that He was buried, and that He rose again the third day according to the Scriptures," (1 Corinthians 15:3-4).

[10] MacArthur, The Gospel According to Jesus, 122.

[11] MacArthur, The Gospel According to Jesus, 210.

[12] John Piper, Future Grace, (Sisters, OR.: Multnomah Publishers, 1995), 151.

Emeritus of Prison Fellowship, Inc. Sproul says this in his book, *Following Christ*, in relation to prayer, "...one of the surest marks of the Christian is his prayer life. One might pray and not be a Christian, but one could not possibly be a Christian and not pray."[13] The implication is clear: if experiential or daily righteousness does not follow a believer through his or her life, then a believer's salvation is in doubt. According to the lordship camp, if believers do not exhibit personal holiness, then they have not submitted to the Lordship of Christ. Additionally, they would conclude that these people are not true believers because they do not exhibit fruit necessarily following "saving faith."

To support their claim lexically, the lordship camp attempts to use the etymological root of the Greek word πιστεύω *(pisteuo)* to justify their theological stance. The summary of their position can be stated thus: πιστεύω *(pisteuo)* is related to πείθω *(peitho)* (meaning to persuade, particularly to move or affect by kind words or motives,[14] obey, be a follower[15]), and, therefore because of the related root *(pith)* in the Greek word etymology between the two words, πιστεύω *(pisteuo)* carries with it the idea of obedience and being a follower. Kenneth Gentry, in his article "The Great Option," states the following regarding the relation between πιστεύω *(pisteuo)* and πείθω *(peitho)* and its root *(pith)*: "...*pith* has the sense of 'to bind' and from this draws the conclusion that the idea of *bind* has a dominant influence on the concept of faith and is of great significance to the Lordship controversy."[16] Making such a strong connection between the root word *pith*, meaning to bind, to πιστεύω *(pisteuo),* meaning to believe or have faith in, seems to be a lexical leap and is a bit far-fetched by any definition of word etymology. James Barr, in his book *The Semantics of Biblical Language,* makes some objective comments regarding the relation between a root and words derived from that root when he states, "...the 'meaning' of a 'root' is not necessarily the meaning of a derived form. Still less can it be assumed that two words having the same root suggest or evoke one another...In many cases the

---

[13] R.C. Sproul, <u>Following Christ</u>, (Wheaton, IL.: Tyndale House Publishers, 1983), 108.

[14]Spiros Zodhiates, <u>The Complete Word Study Dictionary: New Testament</u>, (Chattanooga, TN: AMG Publishers, 1992), 1133.

[15]James Swanson, <u>Dictionary of Biblical Languages With Semantic Domains : Greek (New Testament)</u> (Oak Harbor:Logos Research Systems, Inc., 1997), Electronic ed., S.

[16] Kenneth L. Gentry, "The Great Option: A Study of the Lordship Controversy," *Baptist Reformation Review (BRR)*, no. 5 (Spring 1976): 54.

'root fallacy' comes to much the same thing as 'etymologizing,' i.e., giving excessive weight to the origin of a word as against its actual semantic value...The main point is that the etymology of a word is not a statement about its meaning but about its history; it is only as a historical statement that it can be responsibly asserted, and it is quite wrong to suppose that the etymology of a word is necessarily a guide either to its 'proper' meaning in a later period or to its actual meaning in that period."[17]

Bing also notes that the lordship position distinguishes between *effective* faith, which uses a combination of πιστεύω *(pisteuo)* with a preposition (*pisteuo eis* OR *pisteuo en* OR *pisteuo epi*) that submits to the Lordship of Christ, and mere intellectual assent (*pisteuo* without a preposition), which is *empty* faith.[18] Again, we quote Gentry, who says, "Thus for a Greek-speaking person to say that he believed 'into' (*eis* plus the accusative), or 'upon' (*epi* plus the accusative or dative) someone, it was a strong statement to the effect that he was placing his entire confidence, trust, or hope into that person or grounding it upon his character as revealed to him...The very act of placing faith into Christ must imply submission to Him...Many people may claim to believe Christ (in the sense of *pisteuo* plus the dative case without a preposition), but this is a far cry from placing one's trust wholly in Him."[19]

Unfortunately, for Gentry, the Biblical evidence does not support his assertion that there is a clear distinction between the multiple πιστεύω *(pisteuo)* clauses mentioned above. The different kinds of faith, or distinctions between types of faith, is generally argued from the gospel of John, which uses πιστεύω *(pisteuo)* ninety-eight times. Leon Morris, in his commentary, *The Gospel According to John*, comments on the various constructions of πιστεύω *(pisteuo)* in John by saying, "The conclusion to which we come is that, while each of the various construction employed has its own proper sense, they must not be too sharply separated from one another. Basic is the idea of that activity of believing which takes the believer out of himself and makes him one with Christ. But really to believe the Father or really to believe the facts about Christ inevitably involves this activity.

---

[17] James Barr, <u>The Semantics of Biblical Language</u> (Glasgow: Oxford University Press, 1961), 102-103, 109.

[18] Bing, <u>Lordship Salvation</u>, 18.

[19] Gentry, "The Great Option," 55-56.

Whichever way the terminology is employed it stresses the attitude of trustful reliance on God which is basic for the Christian."[20] The meaning of the word πιστεύω *(pisteuo)* is to believe, have faith in, to trust, and to be firmly persuaded as to something.[21] Built into the meaning of the word is the concept of "relying upon" or "trusting wholly in someone or something." To imply that this word is insufficient by itself to express "true" reliance upon something or someone is to expose a pre-conceived notion regarding the word's meaning.

In addition to the brief points made above, the lordship gospel is incorrect for the following reasons: (1) First, the Bible uses "faith alone" as the only prerequisite for salvation over 160 times in the New Testament.[22] This overwhelming textual evidence supports the free grace view and leaves the lordship camp with much explaining to do as to why the apostles and other New Testament writers did not include the necessary "submission," "commitment," etc. to the gospel presentation. According to the lordship view, one would think and/or expect that the Bible would have 150 references to the message found in Luke 9:23, "...if anyone desires to come after Me, let him deny himself, and take up his cross daily and follow Me." Lordship advocates place more emphasis on this verse, or the teaching in this verse, more than the clear teaching of John 3:16, Acts 16:31, Ephesians 2:8-9, and others. John Piper says, "Saving faith is no simple thing. It has many dimensions. 'Believe on the Lord Jesus Christ' is a massive command. It contains a hundred other things. Unless we see this, the array of conditions for salvation in the New Testament will be utterly perplexing...We must believe on Jesus and receive him and turn from our sin and obey him and humble ourselves like little children and love him more than we love our family, our possessions, or our own life. This is what it means to be converted to Christ. This alone is the way of life everlasting."[23] If John Piper is truly correct here, can anyone be saved? Does anyone do these things perfectly or consistently enough to warrant, merit, or prove that they have eternal life? Of

---

[20] Leon Morris, The Gospel According to John: The New International Commentary on the New Testament (Grand Rapids: William B. Eerdmans Publishing Co., 1971), 337.

[21] Zodhiates, The Complete Word Study New Testament, 4100.

[22] J.B. Hixson, "150+ Verses Proving Justification by Faith Alone," *Not By Works*, last modified December 29, 2009, accessed November 22, 2019,
http://www.notbyworks.org/Salvation-And-Discipleship.

[23] John Piper, Desiring God (Sisters, OR.: Multnomah Publishers, 2003), 65-66.

course, the exegetical "gymnastics" used to sidestep these obvious truths is quite entertaining. MacArthur and friends attempt to tell us what words *really* mean by re-defining words as it suits their cause,[24] and, how what is being said cannot really be *what is being said*.[25]

(2) The Lordship camp does not get the gospel right. Paul clearly defines the gospel of being comprised of two objective truths along with two verifiable proofs in 1 Corinthians 15:1-8 when he says,

"Moreover, brethren, I declare to you the gospel which I preached to you, which also you received and in which you stand, [2] by which also you are saved, if you hold fast that word which I preached to you—unless you believed in vain. [3] For I delivered to you first of all that which I also received: that Christ died for our sins according to the Scriptures, [4] and that He was buried, and that He rose again the third day according to the Scriptures, [5] and that He was seen by Cephas, then by the twelve. [6] After that He was seen by over five hundred brethren at once, of whom the greater part remain to the present, but some have fallen asleep. [7]After that He was seen by James, then by all the

---

[24] "The Greek word for repentance, *metanoia*, literally means 'to think after.' It implies a change of mind, and some who oppose lordship salvation have tried to limit its meaning to that. But a definition of repentance cannot be drawn solely from the etymology of the Greek word... It (Repentance) is much more than a mere change of mind—it involves a complete change of heart, attitude, interest, and direction. It is a conversion in every sense of the word." MacArthur, The Gospel According to Jesus, 47-48. *Interestingly enough, MacArthur was O.K. to solely use the etymology for the Greek word* **kurios** *earlier in his book. However, when the etymology and normal use of the word* **metanoia** *did not suit his purpose, he incorporated a lordship definition for it.*

[25] "But then why does He say, 'No longer do I call you slaves...I have called you friends'? Is He expressly telling them their relationship with Him was now a familiar personal camaraderie between colleagues, rather than a master-slave relationship governed by authority and submission? Does that part of the statement show that He was disclaiming the whole slave metaphor? Not at all. Look at the context. First, He expressly indicates that He had called them slaves—because that is precisely what they were: **douloi**, with Him as their uncontested **kurios**. That relationship, by definition, cannot change. So in verse 15 He is simply saying they were His friends as well as His slaves. And He clearly explains why He makes a differentiation between mere slaves and friends: 'The slave does not know what his master is doing.' In other words, a slave's obedience is implicit, unhesitating; and he is not owed any explanation or rationales from the Master. He is to obey whether he understand why or not." MacArthur, The Gospel According to Jesus, 33. *This was very clear language that MacArthur twisted to prove his point.*

apostles. [8] Then last of all He was seen by me also, as by one born out of due time."

The two objective components of the gospel are (a) Christ died for our sins (v3), and (b) He rose again the third day (v4). The two verifiable proofs are (a) He was buried, proving that He did indeed die, and (b) He was seen by over five hundred people (listed in verses 5-8) after His death, proving that He did indeed come back to life. As was stated previously, the lordship gospel is defined by what man is to "do" rather than what Jesus has done (namely died for our sins and rose again). MacArthur defines the gospel in the following ways in different books at different times over the course of his ministry: "sinners are called to submit to Christ,"[26] "to be a Christian is to be Christ's slave,"[27] "repentance from sin and *total* submission to Christ is a part of the gospel message,"[28] "the heart of the gospel message is you live by dying" (Matthew 16:24-25),[29] "if you want to follow Christ right into heaven, here's the *(gospel)* message: deny yourself, take up your cross, and follow Him," (italics added)[30] "I will abandon all things I think I need for the sake of Christ,"[31] and, finally, "But start preaching the *true* gospel, the hard words of Jesus that call for total and absolute self-denial—the recognition that we're worthy of nothing, commendable for nothing, and that nothing in us is worth salvaging—and that's a lot less popular."[32]

Even though it is not always crystal clear, that the lordship view has confused the focus of the gospel and transferred the attention to man and what man must do rather than on the objective truths of the gospel: (a) Christ died for our sins and (b) rose again on the third day. The lordship view, according to its own description, is supposedly a more God-honoring, Christ-focused gospel than the free grace position. However, the lordship "gospel" does not even need to include the objective facts that Paul clearly states *"is"* the gospel in 1 Corinthians 15. They are indeed teaching *another* gospel, and they must be sharply rejected and opposed (Galatians 1:8-9). The results of

---

[26] MacArthur, Slave, 14.

[27] MacArthur, Slave, 22.

[28] MacArthur, Slave, 74.

[29] John MacArthur, Jr., Hard to Believe: The High Cost and Infinite Value of Following Jesus (Nashville: Thomas Nelson, 2003), 5.

[30] MacArthur, Hard to Believe, 11.

[31] MacArthur, Hard to Believe, 14.

[32] MacArthur, Hard to Believe, 14-15.

their teaching in believers' lives reveal themselves over time and are damaging to their spiritual growth. Paul points out in Colossians 2:6 that individuals' understanding of how they were saved inform the method by which they are to live the Christian life in an acceptable way to the Lord. "As you therefore have received Christ Jesus the Lord, so walk in Him." Much like a home built on a faulty foundation, or with shifting soil, reveals the nature of the foundation through cracks in the walls; the lordship gospel reveals itself to be a faulty foundation on which to build one's Christian life.

CHAPTER 2
Lordship Gospel's Temporal Insecurity[33]

The story is told of a western traveler in the pioneer days who came upon the banks of a wide river one winter night. He had to get across, but there was no bridge. The river was coated with a sheet of ice, but he did not know how safe it was. After much hesitation, he gingerly tested it with one foot, and it held. Night was coming quickly, and he knew he must get across the river. With many fears and with anxious care, he crept out on hands and knees, hoping to evenly distribute his weight on the uncertain ice. When he had painfully and slowly gone some distance, he suddenly heard the sound of horse hooves and joyful singing. There, in the dusk, was a man happily driving a wagon, pulled by a muscular horse, which held a load of coal, across the ice. The man was cheerfully singing as he went. He knew the ice was safe, and he had no fears.

Both of these men were absolutely safe on that ice. The ice was thick and solid. It could have easily born twice that weight. One man was in fear and doubt because he did not know how safe he was and did not realize how solid and thick the ice was. The other man enjoyed his ride across the frozen river because he knew without any doubt that the ice would hold, and the foundation under him was solid and safe.[34] Imagine if a third man screamed from the side of the river, "Watch out! Yes, the ice is thick and solid and able to bear your weight easily; this is true. However, if for some reason you do not step correctly, or, if you do something "wrong," the ice will open a hole, and you will be swallowed up!" This represents the view of the lordship salvationist in regard to the doctrine of eternal security and subsequent doctrine of assurance for the believer. The proponent of lordship salvation's focus tends to be more centralized upon the believer rather than the Savior in whom one believes.

Eternal security, defined, according to Dr. Charles Ryrie, is the work of God, which guarantees that the gift of salvation, once received, is possessed

---

[33] A special thanks to Dr. Dennis Rokser, Senior Pastor of Duluth Bible Church in Duluth, Minnesota for this title.

[34] George Zeller, "Eternal Security: The True Believer is Safe and Secure in Christ Forever!," *Middletown Bible Church*, accessed November 22, 2019, http://middletownbiblechurch.org/salva/salva6.htm,.

forever and cannot be lost.[35] The biblical doctrine of eternal security is thus based on the efficacious work of Christ and is guaranteed to the one who places his or her faith in the Savior and His work alone. The subsequent and related doctrine of assurance could be defined as the realization that a person indeed has eternal life[36], and, as Ryrie says, "…Security is a true fact whether or not that individual has assurance of that fact or not."[37] J. Hampton Keathley III, in his book *ABC's For Christian Growth,* says the following in relation to assurance: "Assurance is the confident realization of that security. It is the realization of what we have in Christ such as eternal life, forgiveness of sin, and being the object of God's personal care as his children. Assurance has to do with our comprehension of the facts and provision of salvation through faith in Christ."[38] Because of many factors (sin, misguided feelings, poor Bible teaching and/or understanding, etc.), the believer's assurance may fluctuate, but the believer's security, in terms of his or her eternal destiny, never does. This is not so, however, in the lordship camp.

In fact, the lordship teaching on eternal security could be adequately summarized by saying, "You are eternally secured *if* you are *really* saved." Is there anything more confusing than that? It is the lordship stance on justification that muddies one's understanding of eternal security and assurance. It is no wonder that the related doctrine of "assurance" is virtually non-existent to the lordship camp. MacArthur puts it this way, "I am committed to the biblical truth that salvation is forever. Contemporary Christians have come to refer to this as the doctrine of eternal security. Perhaps the Reformers' terminology is more appropriate; they spoke of the perseverance of the saints. The point is not that God guarantees Heaven to everyone who professes faith in Christ, but rather that those whose faith is genuine will never totally or finally fall away from Christ. They will persevere in grace unto the very end. Even if they fall into grievous sins or continue in sin for a time, they will never abandon the faith completely."[39] Taking note of this quote, it is interesting to see MacArthur's focus is entirely on man. If one were to count the references to man (9) and the references to God (1) in this

---

[35] Ryrie, So Great Salvation, 137.
[36] Ryrie, So Great Salvation, 137.
[37] Ryrie, So Great Salvation, 137.
[38] J. Hampton Keathley III, ABC's For Christian Growth, (Richardson, TX: Biblical Studies Press, 1996), 21.
[39] MacArthur, The Gospel According to Jesus, 109.

quote, one could clearly see the lordship camp's infatuation with believers "keeping themselves saved" rather than the biblical doctrine of God keeping believers saved. "Now to Him who is able to keep you from stumbling and to present *you* faultless before the presence of His glory with exceeding joy" (Jude 24).

In a question-and-answer period at Grace Community Church in 2017, MacArthur answered three questions that a member from the audience, Joy had.[40] Through tears, Joy asked, "(1) How do I know I am saved if I have blasphemous thoughts? (2) Should I be taking communion if I am not sure I am saved? (3) If I am not chosen, would I even care about being saved?" Joy was clearly struggling with assurance, and it is very telling to see where MacArthur places the focus of his answer - not on the finished work of Jesus Christ but on the way Joy felt! This is what MacArthur had to say to her, "The way you know that you are saved is by your desire. Do you desire to know God?"

"Yes," Joy replied.

"Do you desire that He would know you and love you?" MacArthur asked.

Again, Joy replied, "Yes."

MacArthur went on, "Do you desire to love Him?"

"Yes," she said.

"Do you desire to honor Him?" MacArthur asked.

"Yes," she said.

"Do you desire to obey His word?" MacArthur persisted.

"I do, but I can't do it on my own strength," Joy replied.

MacArthur stated, "Well, of course not! Join the club! That's why we're all here; this is the same with all of us; it's all of grace. Isn't it? It's all of grace." He goes on to say later in the same conversation after discussing Paul's heartfelt cry in Romans 7:24-25, "So, what you're saying to me is essentially the same cry that came out of the noblest of all Christians and that very cry is evidence of the work of God in your heart that that you desire to know God to be loved by God, to love God, to honor God, to obey God and that you know you can't is a statement of a genuine believer…it's about direction, it's

---

[40] John MacArthur, "John MacArthur – Assurance of Salvation," *YouTube* video, 7:09, January 3, 2017, https://www.youtube.com/watch?v=iHivtfyUmMc&t=62s

about affection, it's about love…and He accepts all of us if we love Him and calls on us to love Him more, so you don't want to evaluate the character of your salvation by your failures. You want to assess the genuineness of your salvation by your desires; by what you love, what you long for, what you want. You're here and that says everything! This is not a place for people running from God. This is a place for people running to Him."

Taking note of the mounting contradictions, here are a few to analyze. In his book *Lordship Salvation: The Only Kind There Is!*, Reverend Curtis I. Crenshaw says, "One must believe Jesus is Messiah, God and man in one Person who died for his sins (1 John 4:1-6, 5:1). And if his faith is genuine, he will love righteousness (1 John 2:29), love the brethren (1 John 4:7-8), obey God (1 John 2:3-5)—in other words persevere. If he lacks these, according to 1 John, he must not conclude he is a Christian."[41] Again, it is interesting to note that when a believer is to look for assurance for his or her eternal destiny, the lordship camp noticeably takes the believer's focus **off** the efficacious work of Christ and puts one's focus on one's own works. Because the lordship camp has no problem adding conditions for justification, it follows they would have no problems with adding conditions for maintaining it. MacArthur adds, "Faith obeys. Unbelief rebels. The direction of one's life should reveal whether that person is a believer or an unbeliever. There is no middle ground. Merely knowing and affirming facts apart from obedience to the truth is not believing in the biblical sense. Those who cling to the memory of a one-time decision of 'faith' but lack any evidence of the outworking of faith had better heed the clear and solemn warning of Scripture: 'He who believes in the Son has everlasting life; and he who does not believe the Son shall not see life, but the wrath of God abides on him, (John 3:36).'"[42] R.C. Sproul adds to this when he says, "Unless the believer's sanctification is evidenced by true conformity to the commandments of Christ, it is certain that no authentic justification ever really took place."[43] John Piper adds, "The battle for obedience is absolutely necessary for our final salvation, because the battle for obedience is the fight of faith…I hope you can see that this is a greater gospel than the other one. It's the gospel of God's victory over sin, not just His tolerance of

---

[41] Curtis I. Crenshaw, Lordship Salvation: The Only Kind There Is!, (Memphis: Footstool Publications, 1994), 127.

[42] MacArthur, The Gospel According to Jesus, 193.

[43] Sproul, Following Christ, 329.

sin."[44] "This covenant-keeping condition of future grace does not mean we lose security or assurance…but what it does mean is that almost all future blessings of the Christian life are conditional on our covenant-keeping."[45]

As the contradictions pile up, it is hard to imagine how any genuine believer could be assured of eternal life. When one begins to add things to the Word of God or begins to emphasize things in a greater way than the Bible does, inevitably one begins to speak out of both sides of one's mouth. The sad thing is that one does not realize it. How can one be eternally secure if one's salvation is somehow maintained or proved out through one's works? How can one *actually* know how he or she will behave or act ten years from now - let alone ten minutes from now? How can the Bible unequivocally state that the one who puts his or her faith in Jesus Christ **has** eternal life (i.e., present possession) when one might not have eternal life ten years or ten minutes down the road? According to the lordship camp, would not the Bible itself be guilty of providing "false assurance" to those who do not persevere in the faith?

In a tragic letter from a member of Grace Community Church, which John MacArthur recorded in one of his books, one can see the damaging outcome of the lordship teaching. Consider the following:

Dear John, I've been attending Grace Church for several years. As a result of a growing conviction in my heart, your preaching, and my seeming powerlessness against the temptations which arise in my heart and which I constantly succumb to, my growing doubts have led me to believe that I'm not saved. How sad it is, John, for me not to be able to enter in because of the sin which clings to me and from which I long to be free. How bizarre for one who has had advanced biblical training and who teaches in Sunday School with heartfelt conviction! So many times I have determined in my heart to repent, to shake loose my desire to sin, to forsake all for Jesus only to find myself doing the sin I don't want to do and not doing the good I want to do. After my fiancée and I broke up I memorized Ephesians as part of an all-out effort against sin, only to find myself weaker and more painfully aware of my sinfulness, more prone to sin than ever before, and grabbing cheap thrills to push back the pain of lost love. This occurs mostly in the heart, John, but that's where it counts and that's where we live. I sin

---

[44] Piper, Future Grace, 333.
[45] Piper, Future Grace, 248.

because I'm a sinner. I'm like a soldier without armor running across a battlefield getting shot up by fiery darts from the enemy. I couldn't leave the church if I wanted to. I love the people and I'm enthralled by the gospel of the beautiful Messiah. But I'm a pile of manure on the white marble floor of Christ, a mongrel dog that sneaked in the back door of the King's banquet to lick the crumbs off the floor, and, by being close to Christians who are rich in the blessings of Christ, I get some of the overflow and ask you to pray for me as you think best.[46]

Because this man had been taught that he is supposed to find assurance of salvation in his behavior, he could never find assurance. In fact, no "honest" person can find assurance based on his or her own actions.

This is the reason that the Bible beckons Christians to take their eyes off themselves and this behavior for their assurance and exhorts them to put their eyes on the One who secured their salvation for them. One needs to go no further than Acts 16:30-31, which states, "And he brought them out and said, 'Sirs, what must I do to be saved?' So they said, 'Believe on the Lord Jesus Christ, and you will be saved, you and your household.'" The Philippian jailor was genuinely sincere when he asked this question regarding eternal life, and yet he approached the issue like every un-believer would: what must I **_do_** to be saved. The focus was on him, and not only that, but the Greek word ποιέω (**_poieo_** meaning to do) is found in the present tense indicating continual action. The jailor's question was one of religion. "What must I continually do to be saved?" Religion is defined as humankind working for God or humankind working their way to God. This was Paul's chance to give the Philippian jailer the lordship gospel of faith, commitment, and subsequent obedience to prove his salvation, but Paul does not do that. He says, "Believe on (upon) the Lord Jesus Christ and you will be saved…" The word translated "on" is the Greek word ἐπί (**_epi_**), which means "on, upon, resting upon, upon the ground of, or upon the authority of." A.T. Robertson, considered by many to be the Dean of American biblical-Greek scholars, says of the "ground-meaning" (of ἐπί), "It is 'upon'… ἐπί implies a real resting upon…"[47] The

---

[46] John MacArthur, "The Believer's Assurance," _Grace To You_, last modified 1990, accessed October 25, 2017, https://www.gty.org/library/articles/45ASSURE/a-believers-assurance-a-practical-guide-to-victory-over-doubt.

[47] A.T. Robertson, <u>A Grammar of the Greek New Testament in Light of Historical Research</u>, (Nashville: Broadman Press, 1934), 600.

emphasis here is on the Philippian jailor resting upon another (Jesus Christ) and not on anything that he has to do to be saved. Believe (πιστεύω) is found in the aorist active imperative and, as a result, indicates a command to perform a one-time action. Following this one-time action, the Scriptures says, "You will be saved," which translates the future passive indicative of σῴζω (*sozo*). The indicative mood indicates that this is a fact, and the passive voice indicates that somebody outside of the Philippian jailor would act on him doing the saving (i.e., God). So, one can see from this passage that the believer's eternal security AND the believer's assurance are both based upon the same things: the Work of Christ and the Word of God.

However, this is not so with the lordship camp, as they actually have a two-pronged approach to eternal security and assurance. Lordship advocates would teach that assurance is both objective and subjective. Reverend Crenshaw explains, "Objective assurance refers to a persuasion that the promises in the Gospel are true while subjective assurance refers to one knowing that he personally is a Christian…There is a beautiful balance to the doctrine of assurance, for to hold only to the objective side leads to antinomianism and to maintain only the subjective side leads to legalism."[48] In fact, Crenshaw goes so far as to conclude the following: "Even further, for a man who continues in sin to have personal assurance would be to encourage a hypocrite and confirm him to hell, which is the real danger of this license (*antinomian*) theology. One who is living in sin is not supposed to have personal assurance, for this is part of God's discipline to bring him back in line. The preacher who encourages assurance to such a one will have his blood on his hands and will be severely judged" (italics added).[49] In his effort to criticize what he feels is an unbalanced approach (i.e., maintaining the objective side of assurance), Crenshaw contradicts himself multiple times within this quote. First, he seems to imply that the person referred to **is** a Christian because the implication is that the preacher is not to give him or her assurance as to his or her salvation in order to "bring the sinner back in line," inferring that he or she was "in line" at the start. Additionally, and as Scripture states, God is **not** in the business of disciplining unbelievers, but, rather, He only disciplines believers (see Hebrews 12:5-11). So, in a strange way, Reverend Crenshaw and others in the lordship camp actually endorse the teaching of their Arminian

---

[48] Crenshaw, Lordship Salvation: The Only Kind There Is, 101, 107.
[49] Crenshaw, Lordship Salvation: The Only Kind There Is, 106.

adversaries that one can "lose their salvation" and, subsequently, can regain it.

The irony of this is that the lordship camp would tout their gospel as "God-centered" or "God-centric" and would label the free grace gospel as "man-centered" or "man-centric" when in essence the lordship gospel depends more upon getting oneself saved and keeping oneself saved through commitment, obedience, and lack of sinning. In fact, anytime a person bases one's assurance subjectively on his or her own obedience or lack of sinning, one of two results occur: (1) absolute and total despair (Romans 7:14-25) or (2) complete arrogance and self-righteousness (1 Corinthians 10:12; Galatians 5:13-15). The lordship camp would obviously promote the first result, as it seems to make them feel better about the ***difficulty*** of salvation.[50] Unfortunately, the lordship camp seems oblivious to the second option, as most of the teachers or proponents of this doctrine probably fall into this category. They are arrogant to assume that "they will remain faithful" even 10 minutes from now, let alone for the rest of their lives. Everett Harrison summarizes the lordship dilemma nicely when he says, "The ground of assurance of salvation is endangered if surrender to Christ's lordship is a part of that ground. Instead of looking to the sufficiency of Christ and His work of redemption, one is compelled to look within to see if he has yielded himself to the Son of God. If he is conscious of times in his life when he has denied the lordship of the Master (and who has not? *Including the lordship teachers*) then he must logically question his standing before God" (italics added).[51]

To make matters worse, the lordship doctrine of perseverance of the saints seems to add to this contradictory and self-righteous approach to salvation. In fact, they assert that perseverance in the faith is essential evidence that one's faith is genuine.[52] Because of their doctrine, lordship proponents teach that obedience is automatic in a true believer's life. MacArthur states, "To be clear (*or unclear*), salvation is by faith alone. Yet genuine saving faith is never alone. It inevitably produces 'fruit in keeping with repentance' (Matt. 3:8), thereby evidencing a transformed heart. The one who claims to know Christ yet

---

[50] Many lordship authors make the comment, "Salvation is free, but it will cost you everything," or something to this effect. They seem to like a lot of "teeth" in their gospel and subsequent doctrines of security and assurance.

[51] Everett F. Harrison, "Must Christ Be Lord to Be Savior?—No." *Eternity* 10 (September 1959): 16.

[52] MacArthur, The Gospel According to Jesus, 216.

continues in patterns of unrepentant sin betrays the credibility of his profession of faith (1 John 1:6). By the same token, the one who claims to belong to Christ yet remains wholly enslaved to sin, deceives himself as to his spiritual condition. True slaves of Christ have been liberated from sin and freed to righteousness. Their lives bear witness to that reality…Now they walk in joyful obedience, motivated out of their heartfelt love for the Master" (italics added).[53] MacArthur seems to live in the world of extremes: a believer will be extremely fruitful, or he or she is an unbeliever. This is in direct contrast with what Jesus taught in John 15:2 regarding abiding in the Vine. In verse 2, Jesus implies different levels of fruit-bearing in describing the process of pruning where a vinedresser is in pursuit of "more" fruit. The Bible is clear: there are different levels of fruit-bearing, not a monolithic assembly line production guaranteed in each believer. The very mention of the condition of abiding indicates that the believer's active part in fruit-bearing, which is trusting the Lord, is not guaranteed because the believer must be reminded and commanded to abide in the vine.

In a somewhat ironic twist, one of MacArthur's theological heroes, John Calvin, via his teaching, disagrees with him regarding where a believer should find his or her assurance, as summarized in the following quote, "John Calvin emphatically warned against looking to ourselves, that is, to our works or the fruit of the Spirit, for certainty of our salvation. He taught that we should look to Christ as the objective basis for assurance. To look to ourselves produces doubt and detracts from the saving work of Christ. He rejected the exhortation to self-examination as a dangerous dogma."[54] 1 Corinthians 4:5 says, "Therefore judge nothing before the time, until the Lord comes, who will both bring to light the hidden things of darkness and reveal the counsels of the hearts. *Then each one's praise will come from God.*" Regarding this verse and particularly the last phrase, Dr. Thomas Constable aptly states, "Evidently God will find something in every faithful Christian's life for which to praise him or her on that day. Paul did not just say each servant would receive what he or she deserves but that each would receive some praise."[55] "Although this

---

[53] MacArthur, Slave, 211.

[54] Charles Bell, Calvin and Scottish Theology: The Doctrine of Assurance, (Edinburg: Handsel, 1985), 28.

[55] Thomas Constable, "Notes on 1 Corinthians," *Plano Bible Chapel*, last modified 2019, accessed November 22, 2019, https://www.planobiblechapel.org/tcon/notes/html/nt/1corinthians/1corinthians.htm.

passage does not explicitly teach that every believer will receive some reward, it is nonetheless indirectly suggestive of that fact in its use of ἕκαστος (**hekastos**)."[56]

R.C. Sproul adds, "Some 'evangelicals' are indeed using justification by faith alone as a license to sin; these can only be deemed properly as pseudo-evangelicals. Anyone who has the most rudimentary understanding of justification by faith knows that authentic faith *always* manifests itself in a zeal for obedience. No earnest Christian *can ever have* a cavalier attitude toward the law of God. Though obedience to such laws does not bring justification, the justified person will *surely endeavor* to obey them" (italics added).[57] If one notices the italicized words, Sproul's emphasis is the absolute certainty that a true believer will *always* be faithful. Not only is this <u>not</u> the normal experience of every Christian, but the Bible does <u>not</u> teach this implied sinless perfection either.

However, lordship proponents dance a fine tight rope act regarding the above statement, as the following quote from MacArthur shows, "Pursuing the standard of perfection does not mean we can never fail. It means that when we fail, we deal with it. Those with true faith will fail - and in some cases, fail pathetically and frequently - but a genuine believer will, as a pattern of life, be confessing sin and coming to the Father for forgiveness (1 John 1:9). Perfection is the standard; direction is the test. If your life does not reveal growth in grace and righteousness and holiness, you need to examine the reality of your faith - even if you believe you have done great things in the name of Christ."[58] Thus, according to lordship teachers, true believers will automatically produce a life of obedience and will unreservedly commit everything to the Lord. However, it is alright if they fail a little bit, as long as it is not too frequent or too persistent. In one side of their mouths, they say that unreserved commitment is essential to "prove out" one's salvation, and yet, on the other side of their mouths, they permit and even allow for failure as long as one really did not mean to do it. It is hard to fathom how authors can take such a strong stand using such all-inclusive words as *always, never, nothing, for certain*, etc. when describing the believer's obedience and

---

[56] Sameul L. Hoyt, <u>The Judgment Seat of Christ: A Biblical and Theological Study</u>, (Milwaukee: Grace Gospel Press, 2011), 110.

[57] Sproul, <u>Following Christ</u>, 214-215.

[58] MacArthur, <u>The Gospel According to Jesus</u>, 215.

perseverance and yet allow for some degree of failure as long as the believer's heart is "right." Who defines this? Keathley III makes an excellent point in this regard, "If we depend on works or obedient living to prove our salvation then we are faced with the following dilemma: If we are living obediently now (the supposed proof of salvation), the possibility exists that could change in the future. If later on we cease to live obediently, then that would prove (based on the above premise) that we are not now true Christians in spite of our obedient lifestyle. So present obedience can never really prove our Christianity and thus, we could never have assurance."[59] In fact, notice the personal confusion expressed by another lordship author, John Stott, when he says, "We must surrender absolutely and unconditionally to the lordship of Jesus Christ. We cannot make our own terms. What will this involve? *In detail I cannot tell you.* In principle, it means a determination to forsake evil and follow Christ" (italics added).[60] Yes, in detail nobody can tell the believer exactly what they must do to be saved because the detail of this theology is not biblically based.

Many lordship proponents say, "You do not have to obey perfectly; you just have to want to obey perfectly!" They also say, "True believers will have a desire to forsake sin, and, if they do not, then they must not be true believers." It is all about the motives, or, as MacArthur said above, "Perfection is the standard. Direction is the test." If evaluating a believer's visible good works were not a cloudy enough standard, the real emphasis of lordship teachers in terms of having assurance of one's salvation becomes even more difficult to define. They teach you must look at and evaluate motives, both their own and other people's. This is a slippery slope, and it is not encouraged anywhere in the Bible because "the heart is deceitful above all things, and desperately wicked; Who can know it?"[61] The Bible also says, "For if anyone thinks himself to be something, when he is nothing, he deceives himself."[62] Evaluating something that one cannot see, and something that oftentimes deceives (even the most sincere person) is not a valid or good way to find assurance.

---

[59] Keathley III, ABC's For Christian Growth, 26.
[60] John R.W. Stott, Basic Christianity, (London: InterVarsity Press, 1958), 128.
[61] Jeremiah 17:9.
[62] Galatians 6:3.

Consider another quote from MacArthur illustrating this all-encompassing, exaggerated theology, "Faith is not an experiment, but a lifelong commitment. It means taking up the cross daily, *giving all* for Christ each day with *no* reservations, *no* uncertainty, *no* hesitation. It means *nothing* is knowingly held back, *nothing* purposely shielded from His lordship, *nothing* stubbornly kept from His control" (italics added).[63] The problem with MacArthur's and others' view on this topic is that they do not take into consideration the clear teaching of Scripture that believers do have the ability to walk according to the flesh. By definition, when believers walk according to the flesh, they are living in direct enmity with God. Romans 8:5-7 clearly states this fact, "For those who live according to the flesh set their minds on the things of the flesh, but those *who live* according to the Spirit, the things of the Spirit. For to be carnally minded *is* death, but to be spiritually minded *is* life and peace. Because the carnal mind *is* enmity against God; for it is not subject to the law of God, nor indeed can be." Hence, when believers walk according to the flesh, they will not *give all* for Christ. They will have *reservations*; they will be *uncertain*; they will *hesitate to obey*; they will *knowingly hold things back*; they will *shield* areas of their life from Christ's lordship; and they will *stubbornly seek to maintain control* of their lives. However, because lordship teachers have been burned in relation to seeing other Christians abuse the grace of God, or "fall away," they have overreacted in this area and created a worse degree of error than the error in which they were reacting to. It seems as if MacArthur's theology on this topic is directly related to a few personal experiences he shares in his book *Hard to Believe*. In this book, he details a few close relationships he had with other young men his age where they evangelized together, taught Bible studies, and passionately pursued the Lord. However, when one went off to college, another graduated from college, and the other one graduated from seminary, all three apparently abandoned the faith through their sinful actions.[64] MacArthur labels these men as unbelievers - those who must have never really believed.

However, if obedience is assured in the Christian's life, then New Testament commands to obey become irrelevant and illogical. This is the point that the lordship proponents miss. Subsequently, this impacts their doctrine on security and assurance. Either the New Testament honestly

---

[63] MacArthur, <u>The Gospel According to Jesus</u>, 201.
[64] MacArthur, <u>Hard to Believe</u>, 100-101.

exhorts believers to obedient Christian living, understanding the real possibility of failure, or the strong ethical sections of the Apostles' writings are reduced to logical absurdities.[65]

Consider Ephesians 4:17, which states, "This I say, therefore, and testify in the Lord, that *you should no longer walk* as the rest of the Gentiles walk…" The very exhortation of the verse implies that believers <u>can</u> still walk as the rest of the Gentiles walk! There is no automatic obedience assumed here nor are there any types of distinctions or levels of sin or habitual sin defined here. The clear teaching of Scripture is that when one is saved, he or she *should not live like an unbeliever anymore*; however, the genuine possibility of such is thereby accounted. Ephesians 4:17 is followed by another two chapters filled with Christian conduct describing how a believer, walking in the Spirit, should live his or her life. The emphasis in the Scripture is always *should* and not *will,* whereas the emphasis from the lordship camp is both *should* AND *will*. In other words, the **<u>scriptural</u>** emphasis is on the probability and <u>not</u> the certainty of a godly walk.

This distinction between *should* AND *will* in the area of good works in the believer's life is seen in multiple passages of the New Testament. Romans 6:4 says, "Therefore we were buried with Him through baptism into death, that just as Christ was raised from the dead by the glory of the Father, even so **we also should walk** in newness of life." In describing the believer's new relationship to indwelling sin, and the reason that God took each believer into the death and resurrection of Jesus Christ, Paul concludes that God did this so that "we also should walk in newness of life." Walking in newness of life is the main goal, as a result of one's identification with Christ in His death to sin. But notice the use of the English word "should" in this translation. Is this just a translator's interpretive choice of word, or is there something in the Greek text that indicates something less than 100% certainty? The Greek word translated "we should walk" is the Greek word περιπατέω (*peripateo*), meaning to tread or walk about. The word is used figuratively to describe how one lives or passes their own life.[66] In describing this action, or manner of life, Paul uses the aorist, active, subjunctive form of the word. Paul uses the aorist tense to describe a point in time action, and, since it refers to an ongoing

---

[65] Kevin J. Butcher, "A Critique of *The Gospel According to Jesus*," <u>The Journal of the Grace Evangelical Society 2</u>, (Spring 1989), 43.

[66] Zodhiates, <u>The Complete Word Study New Testament</u>, 4043.

"walk" or manner of life, he is referring to a point in time action now, one moment from now, and then another moment from then, etc. This is what is known as a durative aorist. Dr. Daniel Wallace, Greek Scholar and Professor at Dallas Theological Seminary, in his book *Greek Grammar Beyond the Basics*, illustrates it this way:

> Suppose I were to take a snapshot of a student studying for a mid-term exam in intermediate Greek. Below the picture I put the caption, 'Horatio Glutchstomach *studied* for the mid-term.' From the snapshot and caption all that one would be able to state positively is that Horatio studied for the mid-term. Now in the picture you notice that Horatio has his Greek text opened before him. From this, you cannot say, 'Because the picture is a snapshot rather than a move, I know that Horatio only had his Greek text opened for a split-second!' This might be true, but the snapshot does not tell you this. All you really know is that the student had his Greek text open. An event happened. From the picture you cannot tell for how long he had his text open. You cannot tell whether he studied for four hours straight (durative), or for eight hours, taking a ten-minute break every 20 minutes (iterative)…The snapshot itself cannot tell if the action was momentary, 'once-for-all,' repeated, at regularly recurring intervals, or over a long period of time.[67]

Thus, this aorist is not referring to a singular point in time action but rather to a moment by moment, active decision to walk by faith in the finished work of Jesus Christ, when He took one into His death with Him to sin. Also, what is very significant in Paul's verb form choice is that he uses a subjunctive mood instead of an indicative mood. Wallace defines the indicative mood by stating: "The indicative mood is, in general, the mood of assertion, or presentation of certainty."[68] Wallace distinguishes the subjunctive by stating: "The subjunctive can be said to represent the verbal action (or state) as uncertain but probable…it is better to call it the mood of probability…"[69] William Mounce, a former pastor and Director of the Greek program at Gordon-Conwell Theological Seminary, distinguishes and contrasts the indicative and subjunctive moods by stating: "As it is normally stated, the indicative is the

---

[67]Daniel Wallace, Greek Grammar Beyond the Basics, (Grand Rapids, MI: Zondervan Publishing House, 1996), 555.

[68] Wallace, Greek Grammar Beyond the Basics, 448.

[69] Wallace, Greek Grammar Beyond the Basics, 461.

mood of reality. It states what is…the subjunctive does not describe what is, but what may (or might) be. In other words, it is the mood not of reality but of possibility (or probability)."[70]

This distinction between the indicative and subjunctive mood is the distinction between *should* AND *will* involving good works in the believer's life. If Paul taught what the lordship camp taught regarding good works in the believer's life, he would have used an indicative mood in Romans 6:4, but he did not. Paul, under the inspiration of the Holy Spirit, carefully chose the subjunctive mood to communicate everything is in place, from a divine perspective, for the believer to "walk in newness of life." This is God's desire, and this *should be* the believer's desire as well, but it is not *guaranteed* that the believer will execute this desire consistently. The use of the subjunctive mood as it relates to the desire, but not certainty, of the believer continuing in good works is also found in Titus 3:8, "This is a faithful saying, and these things I want you to affirm constantly, that those who have believed in God *should be careful* (subjunctive mood) to maintain good works. These things are good and profitable to men," and Ephesians 2:10, "For we are His workmanship, created in Christ Jesus for good works, which God prepared beforehand that *we should walk* (subjunctive mood) in them," and Romans 7:4, "Therefore, my brethren, you also have become dead to the law through the body of Christ, that you may be married to another - to Him who was raised from the dead, that *we should bear fruit* (subjunctive mood) to God." So, although good works and bearing fruit is desirable for the Christian, the lordship camp creates a grievous error in emphasizing that these things are guaranteed to happen if someone is a "true" Christian.

As a result of their unscriptural emphasis on the necessary and certain godly walk of "true" believers, the Lordship view creates a theology of "undefinable" terms when it comes to eternal security and the believer's assurance. Dr. Bing summarizes the issue well when he says, "When one's focus is taken off of the person and work of Christ as the object of salvation and placed on the degree of one's own submission, the certainty of attaining salvation falls victim to the subjectivity of human experience. Some lordship advocates speak of only the *willingness* to submit, but this brings the same fate.

---

[70] William D. Mounce, <u>Basics of Biblical Greek</u>, (Grand Rapids, MI: Zondervan Publishing House, 1993), 289.

When does one ever know when he has submitted enough or is willing enough?"[71]

These undefinable terms go on and on throughout lordship writings to the extent that one is left to wonder if **anyone** can know whether or not one is saved before he or she dies. Consider the following samples of "undefinable" terminology used by prominent lordship authors. MacArthur states, "There are times when all of us will stumble into a sin, but if unrepentant sin is the *pattern* of your life, you're not in His kingdom" (italics added).[72] Later in the same book, MacArthur states, "People ask me how to determine whether people are Christians or not…The way you can tell a person is truly a Christian is by *what he desires*. If he *longs* to praise and worship God and Christ, that is evidence of a transformed heart" (italics added).[73] A couple of pages later MacArthur adds, "Look at people who claim to be Christians, and see how *deeply* they worship the Lord. See how they *sing the songs*" (italics added).[74] In his book, *Slave*, MacArthur continues with the ambiguity when he says, "Those who claim to belong to Christ but *persist in patterns of disobedience* betray the reality of that profession" (italics added).[75] In another area of the same book, MacArthur states, "*Loving obedience* is the defining evidence of salvation, such as that the two are *inseparably linked*" (italics added).[76] John Piper, in his book *Future Grace,* adds, "Jesus said, if you don't *fight* lust, you won't go to heaven. *Not that saints always succeed.* The issue is that we *resolve to fight*, not that we succeed flawlessly…But if we don't *fight* lust we lose our soul" (italics added).[77] On the next page, Piper adds, "And the test of whether our faith is the *kind of* faith that justifies is whether it is the *kind of* faith that sanctifies" (italics added).[78] Again, Piper states, "Faith delivers from hell, and the faith that delivers from hell delivers from lust. I do not mean that our faith produces a perfect flawlessness in this life. I mean that it produces a *persevering fight*" (italics added).[79] Yet another lordship proponent, Reverend Curtis

---

[71] Bing, Lordship Salvation, 117.
[72] MacArthur, Hard to Believe, 117.
[73] MacArthur, Hard to Believe, 167.
[74] MacArthur, Hard to Believe, 169.
[75] MacArthur, Slave, 47.
[76] MacArthur, Slave, 92.
[77] Piper, Future Grace, 331.
[78] Piper, Future Grace, 332.
[79] Piper, Future Grace, 332.

Crenshaw, says this: "In the Reformed concept, a lack of personal assurance causes one to run to the Triune God and use the *means of grace*, looking to Christ for *confirmation*, to *produce in him graces* that he cannot produce himself…" (italics added).[80] Reverend Crenshaw also quotes John Owen (1616-1683) who wrote the *Savoy Declaration of Faith and Order*, which used the Westminster Confession of Faith as its guide, when he states, "This certainty is not a bare conjectural and probable persuasion, grounded upon a fallible hope, but an infallible assurance of faith, founded on the blood and righteousness of Christ, revealed in the Gospel, and also upon the *inward evidence* of those graces unto which the promises are made, and on the *immediate witness* of the Spirit, testifying our adoption, and as a fruit thereof, leaving the heart more humble and holy" (italics added).[81]

Hence, to keep a tally on all of the ways one can tell who is and who is not a Christian, the following has to be true, according to the lordship authors quoted above: **(1) One cannot engage in a pattern of unrepentant sin, or one cannot persist in patterns of disobedience and have assurance of one's salvation**. Apparently, one can stumble into sin, but it cannot be a pattern. The problem with this ambiguity is how would the lordship authors define "stumble" because it is obviously an important distinction they are making in the type of sin that would not bring into question one's salvation. "Stumbling" into sin seems to imply an innocent motive - something that happened to someone unexpectantly without pre-meditation. So, that begs the question: Would any type of pre-meditated or intentional sin (i.e., a bad motive) be considered proof that one is not "truly" saved? The "stumbling" type of sin must be the only type of sin that the lordship authors themselves engage in since it appears to be the only "acceptable" type of sin in which one can engage and not have his or her salvation in question. Secondly, what constitutes a "pattern"? Is it twice a year, once a month, once every two weeks, once a week, or every day? The lordship authors cannot define "pattern" because the Bible does not speak of it. They are left to define and clarify how "habitual" is "too habitual," and what constitutes a type of pattern that really brings into doubt one's salvation. This is based upon subjective evaluation by each individual teacher and has no objective basis in the Scriptures. **(2) One has to deeply desire to worship and sing to the Lord.** The only possible

---

[80] Crenshaw, <u>Lordship Salvation: The Only Kind There Is</u>, 105.
[81] Crenshaw, <u>Lordship Salvation: The Only Kind There Is</u>, 111.

reference in the Bible regarding this point is found in Ephesians 5:18-19, which states, "And do not be drunk with wine, in which is dissipation; but be filled with the Spirit, speaking to one another in psalms and hymns and spiritual songs, singing and making melody in your heart to the Lord." However, this is not presented in Ephesians 5 as a "tell-tale" sign of whether or not someone is a Christian, but, rather, whether or not a Christian is walking in the Spirit. To make whether or not one "sings to the Lord" a measurement of whether someone is saved is based upon subjective observation versus objective Scriptural truth. **(3) One has to fight lust and generally have a persevering fight in relation to sin.** This implies that if one is "losing" the battle to lust, then one probably does not have the type of faith that saves. Willingness is cited as the one true evidence that one is "truly" saved or possesses the "type" of faith that saves. Roy Zuck, professor at Dallas Theological Seminary, makes a great point regarding this in his article *Cheap Grace.* He states, "Willingness to do something is not the same thing as actually doing it, and it does not answer the question, 'How much commitment is necessary?' If lordship proponents do not mean a person must surrender *everything* to be saved, then why do they say *all* must be surrendered?"[82] The point is well made that **_willingness_** is just as ambiguous and difficult to define as all of the other lordship terms, such as surrender and commitment because no one can ever give a definitive answer to the question: What does full surrender, full commitment, and full willingness look like? Better yet, the million-dollar question is, "How do you know when/if one's surrender, commitment, and willingness reach the level of acceptability with God?" The simple answer is that **_no one can know for sure_** in the lordship model. By the way, lordship teachers cannot have it both ways: Are they measuring one's visible good works and decrease in sin, OR are they measuring one's deep heart motives? If it is all about good works and a decrease in sin, why do they talk about having the right desire, the right direction, and the proper motives? If it is truly about patterns of sin and good works, then those are measurable. Now, if it is about deep heart motives, then these are things that no human being is qualified to measure. Both of these approaches lead to uncertainty, as it relates to one's assurance of salvation. **(4) One lacking assurance should run to God and pursue the means of grace, and one should gain assurance through inward evidences of**

---

[82] Roy B. Zuck, "Cheap Grace?," <u>Kindred Spirit</u> (KS), 13 (Summer 1989): 6-7.

grace and immediate witness of the Holy Spirit. Again, the problem with this phraseology is that it is impossible to clearly define. What exactly are the "means of grace," so that a genuine believer could know what to pursue? Additionally, when one is gaining assurance through "inward evidences of grace" and "immediate witness of the Holy Spirit," the lordship camp sets each individual believer up to be his or her own judge and jury. In other words, one's assurance is based upon one's own spiritual measuring stick, which is extremely subjective. In fact, one cannot imagine a more subjective theology than what is presented. This is truly a "Burger King" theology where "Everyone Gets Their Own Way." Lordship proponents have left it to themselves to determine God's acceptance of them based on which sins, how many sins, and how often they commit sin. They clearly define and subjectively apply certain criteria and standards in their own lives that they can indeed meet or achieve. Because there has been no bar set by the Scriptures in these areas of ambiguity, each lordship proponent is left to determine that "bar" for themselves, all the while judging others in relationship to their own standards. This is why Paul rightly states that even he would not engage in self-evaluation. In 1 Corinthians 4:3-5 he says, "But with me it is a very small thing that I should be judged by you or by a human court. In fact, *I do not even judge myself.* For I know of nothing against myself, yet I am not justified by this; but He who judges me is the Lord. Therefore, judge nothing before the time, until the Lord comes, who will both bring to light the hidden things of darkness and reveal the counsels of the hearts. Then each one's praise will come from God (italics mind)."

Unfortunately, when this personal and subjective bar is established, incorrect theology follows. Consider MacArthur's direct contradiction of Scripture when he states, "Though Christians do fall into sin from time to time, through their own disobedient choices, *they are never again the slaves of sin* as they were before being rescued by Christ and set free. *Sin no longer has the power to control them*" (italics added).[83] Romans 6:12-13 clearly implies that the believer **_can_** "let sin reign in our mortal bodies," and the believer **_can_** "present our members as instruments of unrighteousness." If this does not imply the sin nature's ability to control the believer, who is yielding to its sinful desires/enticements, what could it be saying? The fact that Paul uses two present active imperatives to tell the believer what not to do indicates that the

---

[83] MacArthur, <u>Slave</u>, 202.

believer has the ability to listen to Paul or not to listen to him. In fact, many times the present active imperative can indicate a command to stop an action **already in progress.** Wallace writes about the present imperative plus μὴ (**me**), which we have in Romans 6:12, and categorizes this combination as "Cessation of Activity in Progress" or Progressive. He goes on to say, "Here the idea is frequently progressive, and the prohibition is of the 'cessation of some act that is already in progress.' It has the idea, *Stop continuing.*[84] The idea communicated by Paul to the believers in Rome could be two-fold: (1) Stop continuing to allow yourself to be dominated by the sin nature through the presentation of your members, or (2) From this moment forward stop presenting your members to the sin nature because you will be dominated by it. Most likely, both emphases can be found in Paul's exhortations.

What is the scriptural "bar" that lordship proponents appeal to in their theology of assurance? Although not all-inclusive, it appears that some of the more popular proof texts are Matthew 7:15-23 and Galatians 5:19-21. In the Matthew 7 passage, Jesus is ending his famous Sermon on the Mount. Although dispensational distinctions could be made regarding this passage, for the sake of pure exegesis, the text will be dealt with independent of them. In the first section of this passage (verses 15-20), Jesus is teaching about false prophets, and how one is to recognize them. According to Jesus, the false prophets are "ravenous wolves," who present themselves in sheep's clothing. This is an apparent reference to their intended deceptiveness in regard to their intentions. In much the same way as the Old Testament encouraged the Israelites to recognize true and false prophets, Jesus encourages those listening to His message to examine the false prophets' fruit. Deuteronomy 18:20-22 says, "But the prophet who presumes to speak a word in My name, which I have not commanded him to speak, or who speaks in the name of other gods, that prophet shall die.' And if you say in your heart, 'How shall we know the word which the LORD has not spoken?'—when a prophet speaks in the name of the LORD, if the thing does not happen or come to pass, that *is* the thing which the LORD has not spoken; the prophet has spoken it presumptuously; you shall not be afraid of him." The question in Matthew 7 then becomes: "What is the 'fruit' that Jesus speaks of in regard to the false prophets?"

In his book *Studies in the Sermon on the Mount*, D. Martyn Lloyd-Jones, a well-known Welsh minister and theologian, who pastored the Westminster Chapel

---

[84] Wallace, <u>Greek Grammar Beyond the Basics</u>, 724.

in London for 30 years, summarizes the two major schools of thought when he says, "There have been two main schools of thought with regard to this statement about the false prophets, and some of the great names in the history of the Church are found on each side. The first is the school which says that this is a reference only to the teaching of the false prophets…the other group, however, disagrees entirely. It says that this reference to the false prophets really has nothing at all to do with teaching, that it is purely a question of the kind of life that these people live."[85] The Scriptures clearly teach that "fruits" can refer to both works (Matthew 3:8; 13:23) and words (Matthew 12:33-37). So, in essence, the answer is probably a little bit of both. However, and what is fascinating about this passage, is to see lordship teachers try to maintain good hermeneutics, all the while trying to import an added emphasis to the text in order to support their lordship theology. Their lordship theological emphasis becomes the faithfulness of individual believers to produce genuine works as proof of their salvation. Many lordship teachers stick pretty true to the sound interpretation of the text by teaching that this passage communicates how one can recognize a "false prophet" (a false teacher). However, once the proper interpretation is communicated, the teachers veer into a vacuum-like vortex - encompassing all believers in this one catch-all test…*by their fruits you shall know them.* Kenneth Gentry in his article, *The Great Option: A Study of the Lordship Controversy,* says this about the passage: "In verses 15-20, He warns that false prophets are everywhere seeking to destroy the believer (*good interpretation*). The method of determining who is a true "sheep" and who is not is by observing their fruit, i.e., their life pattern (*bad interpretation*)" (italics added).[86] From Gentry's comments, it appears that the passage at hand is dealing more with how one can tell whether someone is a "true sheep" rather than a "true teacher." The thrust of Jesus' message in this section is focused on the false teacher, NOT the ones listening to the message. In relationship to this passage, Lloyd-Jones agrees with Gentry when he states, "…we must emphasize the great principle which our Lord is here inculcating. It is that to be a Christian is something central to personality, something vital and fundamental. It is not a matter of appearance on the surface either with regard to belief of life. In using this picture of the character, the nature, the

---

[85] D. Martyn Lloyd-Jones, <u>Studies in the Sermon on the Mount</u>, (Grand Rapids: Eerdmans Publishing Company, 1971), 242.

[86] Gentry, "The Great Option," 71.

real essence of these trees and the fruit which they produce, our Lord is placing very great emphasis upon that. And surely this is the point which we must always be looking for in ourselves and in others…we must grasp this principle, that to be a Christian means a change in a man's very life and nature."[87]

Unfortunately, this type of interpretation has been going on for quite a while. Lloyd-Jones refers to the Puritans' teaching regarding this section, "The Puritans were very fond of dealing at great length with what they called 'temporary believers.' They meant by that, people who seemed to come under the influence of the gospel, and who gave the appearance of being truly and soundly converted and regenerate. Such people said the right things and there was a change in their lives; they appeared to be Christian. But the Puritans called them 'temporary believers' because those people gave clear, unmistakable evidence afterwards that they had never truly become Christian at all."[88] Although it is clear from the verses following Matthew 7:15-20 that there are people who think they are saved but are not, the "fruits" identified in verse 20 are not describing false Christians in general but rather false teachers. This passage, therefore, only teaches how to discern a false prophet not how to discern whether one is saved[89] and should not be used as such by lordship teachers. Interestingly enough, if the passage is referring to a necessary change of life to determine a true believer, Jesus' analogy breaks down. This is because of His first description of them – they "come to you in sheep's clothing." In other words, they externally look like true sheep! Their externals, their works, and their deeds all look like the real thing! This is the exact opposite of what lordship teachers take away from this passage.

The next section in Matthew 7 is an even more popular proof text for the lordship camp in relation to the doctrine of security and assurance. In context, 7:21-23 is chiefly concerned with the false prophets discussed in 7:15-20 (cf. verse 22—they "prophesied"). Their prophetic "ministries" of good works are acknowledged (verse 22) but have no merit in the day of final judgment.[90] However, it would be too dogmatic to claim that Jesus is "only" referring to the false prophets in this passage. By implication, verses 21-23 could include

---

[87] Lloyd-Jones, <u>Studies in the Sermon on the Mount</u>, 252-253.
[88] Lloyd-Jones, <u>Studies in the Sermon on the Mount</u>, 254.
[89] Bing, <u>Lordship Salvation</u>, 41.
[90] Bing, <u>Lordship Salvation</u>, 41.

false professors (people who think they are saved, but who have never put their faith alone in Jesus Christ and His work on the cross for them).

Now, as one gets into the passage, it is amazing to note the lordship teachers' emphasis in these verses. As Bing rightly states, "This passage is also quoted by lordship proponents as evidence that faith which saves must manifest itself in works of obedience. Given their understanding, the passage would actually teach against using works as proof of salvation, because the works performed in verse 22 do not reveal the professors' true spiritual condition as shown by the subsequent rebuke (verse 23)."[91] Consider MacArthur's statements regarding verse 21, "It is not the ones who say, and it is not the ones who hear. It is the ones who what? Who do. In other words the Lord is saying, if you do not live a righteous life, I don't care what you say or what you hear, You're deceived."[92] "But the bottom line is this, with all of your false assurance, with all your failure to self-examine, with all this fixation on religious activity and with the fair exchange principle in operation, the bottom line that you'd better examine is this, *do you live in total obedience to the Word of God?* And when you disobey it, is there a sense of conviction and remorse that draws you to confess it to God? And if that isn't there, there's a fair question about whether you're even a Christian. Because the one who comes into the Kingdom, verse 21 says, is the one not who says, but the one who *does*" (italics added).[93] "The *only thing* that makes you acceptable to God is a *pattern of obedience* to the Word of God, that is the product of repentance and genuine faith in Jesus Christ and truly abandoning your life in obedience to His lordship" (italics added).[94] The sad fact with these quotes from MacArthur is that he sounds more like the false professors who are rebuked in verse 23 than he does Jesus. The false professors' _main emphasis_ is their works, or what they _did_ for the Lord, (much like MacArthur). This is nothing less than a "works salvation," and, as Jesus notes in verse 23, good works do not save and are in fact viewed as lawlessness and filthy rags (see Isaiah 64:6). MacArthur truly misses the point when he states, "Jesus sends away those

---

[91] Bing, Lordship Salvation, 41.

[92] John MacArthur, "Empty Words," *Grace to You*, last modified June 8, 1980, accessed January 20, 2012, http://www.gty.org/resources/sermons/2255/empty-words,

[93] MacArthur, "Empty Words."

[94] John MacArthur, "Saved or Self Deceived part 2," *Grace to You*, last modified November 11, 2007, accessed January 8, 2012, http://www.gty.org/resources/sermons/80-327/saved-or-selfdeceived-part-2.

who falsely claim to know Him because they 'practice lawlessness' (Matthew 7:23). Instead of doing the will of God and living by these righteous principles Jesus explained in the Sermon on the Mount, they live sinfully."[95] It is interesting to note that the people's "sinful lives" are not mentioned anywhere in this passage but rather their good works are. However, Jesus likens their good works to lawlessness because no amount of good works will ever get anyone into Heaven. MacArthur assumes that because Jesus rebukes them and says that He never knew them, that they lived sinfully, or that they lived morally corrupt lives. However, the text never says that.

Additionally, lordship teachers read too much into the phrase "Lord, Lord" in verse 21, as Lloyd-Jones states, "He is referring to people who are right in their doctrine concerning His nature and about His Person, to people who have recognized Him, and who come to Him, and say 'Lord, Lord.' They say the right things to Him, they believe the right things about Him."[96] MacArthur adds, "They're saying, we know You're God, we know You're Jehovah, we accept all that Your deity involves, Your virgin birth, miraculous life, substitutionary death, powerful resurrection, intercession, second coming, they are respectful, they are orthodox, they use the right terms, the right attitudes."[97] To say that both these men impregnated the meaning of the words "Lord, Lord" would be an understatement; they not only impregnated it but did so with triplets! The point of these professors using "Lord, Lord" is that they are using a respectful term akin to "teacher" or "sir." It was a title of admiration in Jesus' day, and Jesus' point was that not everyone who just _says_ "Lord, Lord" will enter the kingdom of Heaven. The one prerequisite for entering the kingdom of Heaven is "doing the will of My Father in Heaven." The question naturally must be asked: "What is the will of the Father?" For the Jew in Jesus' day, the answer would be faith in God's Word (i.e., the promises made to the patriarchs involving the covenants) and faith in the Promised Deliverer (from Genesis 3:15). The answer, in short, would be faith. For those in the present day, after Jesus Christ, the Lamb of God, dealt with the sin problem forever through His own death on the Cross, the answer is still the same but with a different object: faith in God's Word and faith in Jesus Christ and His work on the Cross. John 6:28-29 says, "Then they said

[95] MacArthur, Hard to Believe, 103.
[96] Lloyd-Jones, Studies in the Sermon on the Mount, 263.
[97] MacArthur, "Empty Words."

to Him, 'What shall we do, that we may work the works of God?' Jesus answered and said to them, 'This is the work of God, that you believe in Him whom He sent.'"

The relationship between John 6:28-29 and Matthew 7:21-23, regarding word choice, is interesting to note. The word translated "do" in John 6:28 is the same Greek word translated "does" in Matthew 7:21. It is the Greek word ποιέω *(poieo)*, which simply means to make, do, expressing action either as completed or continued. Additionally, the word translated "work" in John 6:28 is the same word translated "practice" in Matthew 7:23. It is the Greek word ἐργάζομαι *(ergazomai)*, which simply means to work or labor. The use of these two words in these two different contexts show that Jesus references the only acceptable "work" to God, which is believing in Him. Thus, when Jesus speaks of "doing the will of God" in Matthew 7:21 as the qualification of entrance into the kingdom of Heaven, He most certainly is speaking of faith in Himself, as all other "doing" is unacceptable in His sight, as it relates to entrance into Heaven (Ephesians 2:8-9). Constable agrees when he states, "During Jesus' ministry doing the will of God boiled down to believing that Jesus was the Messiah and responding appropriately."[98] The "lawlessness" spoken of is not external sin, as the lordship camp would have one believe, but rather the sin of thinking that doing good works is good enough for one to gain entrance into the kingdom of Heaven. Even though these people appeared to be doing "good works," their righteousness was like filthy rags (see Isaiah 64:6) and, therefore, classified as lawless.

In Galatians 5:19-21, lordship authors seem to focus on the works of the flesh being indicators of a professing believer who is not truly saved. According to them, the people mentioned in the passage are either professing believers, who through their life and actions *prove* they were never really saved, or they are just your average run of the mill unbeliever. Interestingly enough, although MacArthur seems to maintain a somewhat proper exegesis in Matthew 7:15-20 regarding the fruit referring to false teachers, in his Galatians commentary, he uses Matthew 7:16-18 to show that true believers will bear fruit, and one can know if someone's conversion is genuine by his or her fruit. MacArthur states, "A believer's sonship to God and citizenship in His

---

[98] Thomas Constable, "Notes on Matthew," *Plano Bible Chapel*, last modified 2019, accessed   November   22,   2019, https://www.planobiblechapel.org/tcon/notes/html/nt/matthew/matthew.htm.

kingdom (cf. verse 21) are manifested by the fruit the Spirit produces in his life. 'You will know [men] by their fruits,' Jesus said. 'Grapes are not gathered from thorn bushes, nor figs from thistles, are they? Even so, every good tree bears good fruit; but the bad tree bears bad fruit. A good tree cannot produce bad fruit,' nor can a bad tree produce good fruit' (Matt. 7:16-18).'"[99] Thus, MacArthur's inconsistent hermeneutics result in his exegesis on the Matthew passage referring only to the false teachers in Matthew 7. However, because it serves the purpose of his lordship theology, he misuses the Matthew passage as a proof text to prove his exegesis of Galatians 5:19-21 referring to professing believers whose faith is not genuine. This is a case where he uses theological hermeneutics rather than a normal, consistent, objective hermeneutic. MacArthur's overarching interpretation of this passage is found in his commentary on Galatians:

Because the list of sins is so all encompassing and the warning so severe, this passage has caused many believers to doubt their salvation. Such fears have been compounded by the unfortunate rendering of the King James Version: 'they which do such things.' 'Who hasn't done some of those things?' people wonder. 'What Christian can claim he has not committed a single one of those sins since he was saved? Who could possibly enter the kingdom of God if committing just one of those sins keeps him out?' The key word in Paul's warning is practice, which translates a present active participle of **prasso**, indicating durative, ongoing action. It is the continual, habitual practice of such things that marks a person as unregenerate and therefore barred from entrance into the kingdom of God. Scripture always assesses a person's character on the basis of his common, habitual actions, not his occasional ones. People who habitually indulge in sin show themselves to be enemies of God, whereas those who habitually do good show themselves to be His children. The unregenerate person occasionally does humanly good things, the regenerate person occasionally falls into sin. But the basic character of the unregenerate is to practice the evil deeds of the flesh and of the regenerate person to bear the good fruit of the Spirit.[100]

The main issue with MacArthur's interpretation of the word πράσσω (**prasso**) and his subsequent applications is something that was discussed

---

[99] John MacArthur, Jr., The MacArthur New Testament Commentary: Galatians, (Chicago: Moody, 1987), 164.

[100] MacArthur, The MacArthur New Testament Commentary: Galatians, 162-163.

earlier - how does one biblically define when sin is so "habitual" that one does not possess eternal life? Additionally, another question arises from MacArthur's comments - how does one differentiate biblically between "habitual" sins and "occasional" sins, as MacArthur seems to do in regard to true Christians "occasionally" falling into sin versus unbelievers who "habitually" sin?

Rather than trying to define something that the Bible does not clearly emphasize, it would be wise to find an alternate interpretation that is in line with other Scriptures. So, who is Paul discussing in this list? Paul uses this terminology to refer to those who are unsaved…this is a life characterized by nothing other than this list. The fact that MacArthur brought out that πράσσω *(prasso)* in verse 21 is a present active participle is a good observation. It does indeed indicate ongoing, durative action. To understand the meaning of πράσσω *(prasso)*, it may be beneficial to contrast its meaning with another Greek word ποιέω *(poieo)*. Whereas ποιέω *(poieo)* means "to make or to do"[101] - it emphasizes the accomplishment of something - πράσσω *(prasso)* means "to do, make. Expressing an action as continued or not yet completed, what one does repeatedly, continually, habitually"[102]—it emphasizes the process whereby something is accomplished. A definite course of conduct is intended to be reflected in πράσσω *(prasso)*. Romans 1:29-32 provides a good contrast of the two words (especially verse 32) within the same context and utilizes a similar list as Galatians 5:19-21. "Who, knowing the righteous judgment of God, that those who practice (πράσσω) such things are deserving of death, not only do (ποιέω) the same but also approve of those who practice (πράσσω) them" (Romans 1:32). This passage clearly seems to teach that one who continually practices such sinful behavior as the list mentioned in Galatians 5 and in Romans 1 is living like an unsaved person. However, because this list characterizes the habitual and durative actions of an unbeliever, it is a leap to assume that these actions could not or would not at times characterize a Christian's life. In fact, if one were to agree with MacArthur's exegesis of this passage, one would be forced to question whether or not the apostle Paul was saved, because in Romans 7:15, 19, he uses the word πράσσω *(prasso)* in relationship to himself regarding sin in his life. "For what I am doing, I do not understand. For what I will to do, that I

---

[101] Zodhiates, <u>The Complete Word Study New Testament</u>, 4160.
[102] Zodhiates, <u>The Complete Word Study New Testament</u>, 1209.

do not practice (πράσσω); but what I hate, that I do…For the good that I will *to do,* I do not do; but the evil I will not *to do,* that I practice (πράσσω)" (Romans 7:15, 19). So, in utilizing MacArthur's hermeneutic and conclusion in Galatians 5 with the word **πράσσω** *(prasso),* one would have to assume that Paul, at least at this point in his life, was not truly saved. Paul's self-admitted "fruit" or lack thereof would condemn him as a false professor through the lens of lordship theology. Why is Paul warning the Galatian believers? Paul is clearly warning believers to recognize when they are walking after the flesh and then to avoid it. His point is for them to look at and remember the outcome for unbelievers…why would they want to associate with that? By implication, for Paul to warn them not to practice the works of the flesh implies that they have the ability to practice the works of the flesh.

For the lordship camp, it is quite acceptable to say that in order for someone to be saved, one must **really** be saved. The apparent contradictions aside, the truth of the matter is no lordship teacher could ever teach with sincerity of heart that someone is truly saved. To maintain doctrinal consistency, lordship teachers would have to teach that one "might have" eternal life because their teaching on perseverance results in not truly knowing. The Apostle John clearly wanted believers to have sure assurance: "These things I have written to you who believe in the name of the Son of God, ***that you may know*** that you ***have eternal life***, and that you may *continue to* believe in the name of the Son of God." If the gospel is faulty (i.e. the lordship gospel), there is no security that God can provide because one's salvation is dependent upon him or her keeping it. Thus, there can never be assurance because one never knows if he or she has done enough to keep him or herself saved.

CHAPTER 3
Set Apart – But Not Really!?

It is interesting to note the differences and similarities between both the lordship view and the free grace view when it comes to the topic of sanctification. Ironically enough, their definitions are quite similar. Consider John MacArthur's textbook definition of sanctification: "The verb ἁγιάζω (**hagiazo**) means to separate, to set apart from…so when we see sanctify or sanctification or holy or holiness, all of those come from the same root. They all have the idea of being separated, set apart."[103] Charles Ryrie, in his book *So Great Salvation*, states, "The word *sanctify* basically means 'to set apart.' It has the same root as the words *holy* and *saint*."[104] Charlie Bing, in his article *Sanctification: Whose Work Is It?*, defines sanctification this way: "The Bible commonly uses the term *sanctify* (the same Greek word behind the words *sanctification, saint, and holy*) to mean set apart from sin to God, to be holy."[105]

In addition to the similar definitions, both lordship writers and free grace writers tend to agree that there are three aspects to sanctification. MacArthur says, "First of all, there are several aspects to sanctification, three of them, and I want you to understand them. Number one is what we can call **positional sanctification**; positional. Or we could call it official sanctification. Or sanctification of one's state before God. This feature of sanctification, this component or element is past…it's a past aspect…the second one, the middle one, (is) **experiential sanctification**. And that's where we live, folks, right now… (this one) fluctuates. Now there is a third…aspect of sanctification you need to understand, we'll call it **ultimate sanctification**; ultimate…Ultimate sanctification is a future aspect."[106] Bing, using almost the exact same terminology as MacArthur, summarizes the three aspects this way: "A Christian's sanctification has three aspects: past

---

[103] John MacArthur, "A Prayer for Complete Sanctification," *Grace to You*, Last modified June 23, 1991, accessed February 10, 2012, http://www.gty.org/resources/sermons/52-35/a-prayer-for-complete-sanctificationm.

[104] Ryrie, So Great Salvation, 150.

[105] Charlie Bing, "Sanctification: Whose Work Is It?," *Grace Life*, accessed November 22, 2019, http://www.gracelife.org/resources/gracenotes/?id=50&lang=eng.

[106] MacArthur, "A Prayer for Complete Sanctification."

(positional justification), present (progressive sanctification), and future (perfect glorification)."[107]

What then is the problem with lordship salvation in regard to the doctrine of sanctification? If the lordship teachers have their definitions correct, how could their lordship gospel impact sanctification in a negative way? As one will see, having the same definitions does not always guarantee the same interpretation. Pastor Dennis Rokser rightly comments, "It is my contention that since the Bible is like a fine piece of tapestry, when you twist the Bible in one area, other areas of doctrine or interpretation are prone to be affected for the sake of harmony and consistency. This results in a classic case of one's theology driving the bus of his interpretation of Scripture."[108] Because each side, and every person on earth tends to bring his or her "theological glasses" to the table when looking at the doctrines of the Bible, one must be careful, thoughtful, and conscientious with his or her exegesis in every area, including sanctification. In fact, Kenneth Gentry, a lordship author aptly summarizes the differences in both sides' approach to sanctification when he says, "Can any two opinions be any more diametrically opposed?...If more time and space were available [*in his article*], a survey of the doctrine of sanctification would prove invaluable; the two camps disagree unreservedly in that area as well." (*italics mine*)[109]

The first and most glaring difference between the lordship view and the free grace view is in the area of what the Bible calls the "carnal" Christian. For the lordship camp, MacArthur accurately represents their view when he states, "The tragic result is that many people think it is fairly normal for Christians to live like unbelievers. As I noted…contemporary theologians have devised an entire category for this type of person - the 'carnal Christian.' Who knows how many unregenerate persons have been lulled into a false sense of spiritual security by the suggestion that they are merely carnal? Please do not misunderstand me. Christians can and do behave in carnal ways. But nothing in Scripture suggests that a real Christian might pursue a lifestyle of unbroken indifference or antagonism toward the things of God."[110]

---

[107] Bing, "Sanctification: Whose Work Is It?"

[108] Dennis Rokser, "Examining Lordship Salvation Pt.10," *Grace Family Journal* Vol. 12, No. 60 Winter (2009).

[109] Gentry, "The Great Option," 69.

[110] MacArthur, <u>The Gospel According to Jesus</u>, 138.

Likewise, Reformed Pastor Walter Chantry states the following in his book *Today's Gospel, Authentic or Synthetic?*: "In a panic over this phenomenon [worldly Christians], the evangelicals have invented the idea of 'carnal Christians.' These are said to be folks who have taken the gift of eternal life without turning from sin. They have 'allowed' Jesus to be their Savior; but they have not yielded their life to the Lord."[111] The lordship camp's objection to the idea of a carnal Christian is not only practical but also theological. They believe that it encourages sin and gives false assurance to someone who has not really made the necessary surrender or commitment to the lordship of Christ. The possibility of a carnal Christian is seen as a direct attack on the lordship gospel.[112]

Furthermore, an even stronger statement is made by lordship teacher Paul Washer in regard to the carnal Christian: "God's work of sanctification is the evidence that He's truly justified a man. There is no such thing as a continuously carnal Christian. It is not in the Bible. It is not in Church history. It is a fabrication of American Christianity. And of course, we have to have it because it's the only way we can explain that the great majority of most of our churches are carnal and worldly."[113]

However, it seems clear that the free grace side of the sanctification argument actually possesses a clearer defense, for the Bible does use the term "carnal" when describing believers. Ryrie says this: "Do the Scriptures indicate that both unbelievers and believers can be called carnal? I think so…Obviously, such a designation for some Christians is not a fabrication; it is a scriptural teaching (1 Corinthians 3:1-4)."[114] Pastor Dennis Rokser agrees and says somewhat sarcastically, "Apparently the apostle Paul had not read the writings of lordship teachers, for he clearly believed in the reality of carnal Christians! [speaking of 1 Corinthians 3:1-4]"[115]

In 1 Corinthians, Paul identifies three anthropological categories from 2:14-3:4. Those categories are: (1) natural man (2:14), (2) spiritual man (2:15-

---

[111] Walter J. Chantry, Today's Gospel: Authentic or Synthetic?, (Carlisle, PA: The Banner of Truth Trust, 1970), 54.

[112] Bing, Lordship Salvation, 177-178.

[113] Paul Washer, "Is There Such a Thing as a Carnal Christian?" *YouTube* video, 10:05, December 30, 2007, http://www.youtube.com/watch?v=WBl568p7aSY.

[114] Ryrie, So Great Salvation, 60-61.

[115] Dennis Rokser, "Examining Lordship Salvation Pt. 6," *Grace Family Journal* Vol. 11, No. 56 Winter (2008).

3:1), and (3) carnal man (3:1-3:4). The natural man ψυχικός (*psuchikos*)
comes from a root word meaning "soul" and could be further defined as the
immaterial life held in common with animals.[116] In the period around and after
500 BC, ψυχή (*psuche*), the root word, was commonly used as an omnibus
term for human thought, will, and emotion and also for the essential core of
man, that can be separated from his body and does not share in the body's
dissolution.[117] Additionally, the word is used in Acts 27:22 of men's lives when
Paul says, "And now I urge you to take heart, for there will be no loss of *life*
(ψυχή) among you, but only the ship."

In other words, ψυχή (*psuche*) is not speaking of the human body
but rather the human life — the life one is given at conception. Because the
suffix "ikos" is added to this word, it communicates that the ψυχή (*psuche*)
is the dominating factor in a person's life. The Lexham Theological
Wordbook describes ψυχικός (*psuchikos*) as being "governed by the soul."[118]
The idea communicated is that this type of person is governed by this natural
human condition, which is the state of every man or woman born on this
earth. It is the life associated with and related to the First Adam, and,
therefore, by position, it is condemned before God.

Jude 19 uses this same word (*psuchikos*) to describe unbelievers as
those who do not have the Spirit of God. Thus, when Paul speaks of the
natural man, he is referring to the unsaved man, as evidenced by what is true
of him in this passage — he does not receive the things of the Spirit of God
because they are foolishness to him; he cannot know them because these
things are only spiritually discerned. It is important to take note of the
distinction that Paul makes in anticipation of his description of the
Corinthians as "carnal." Paul not only says that natural man <u>does not</u> receive
spiritual things, but he <u>cannot</u> (i.e., he is unable) know spiritual things. The
word used is δύναμαι (*dunamai*), meaning "to be able, have power, by virtue
of one's own ability and resources."[119] As will be seen later, this is a difference
AND similarity between natural and carnal man: the natural man does not
receive spiritual things because he *cannot (he is unable to)* know spiritual things,

---

[116] Zodhiates, The Complete Word Study New Testament, 5591.

[117] G. Kittel, G. W. Bromiley & G. Friedrich, Ed., *Vol. 9: Theological dictionary of the New Testament,* (electronic ed.), (Grand Rapids, MI: Eerdmans, 1964), 611.

[118] Douglas Mangum, Derek R. Brown, Rachel Klippenstein, Rebekah Hurst, *Lexham Theological Wordbook*, (Bellingham, WA: Lexham Press, 2013), *Soul*.

[119] Zodhiates, The Complete Word Study New Testament, 485.

as he is thoroughly unequipped with the proper divine resources to do so; and the carnal man can receive spiritual things, but he *cannot (he is unable to)* receive spiritual things in a carnal state. In other words, the carnal Christian cannot receive spiritual things because, although he possesses the divine resources to do so, he does not take advantage of them. The natural man does not have the ability to receive spiritual things because he lacks divine resources, and the carnal Christian has the ability to do so, due to the divine resources he possesses, but he does not take advantage of them.

The next category of man that Paul identifies in this passage is the spiritual man πνευματικός (*pneumatikos*), which carries the basic meaning of spirit, or spiritual. Both Galatians 6:1 and 1 Peter 2:5 use this word to describe believers. Based upon the description of the person in this passage, it would appear that Paul is using the term to describe a believer here as well. The believer is described the following ways: one who judges all things while he (or she) himself is not judged, one who has the mind of Christ, and one who is capable of eating and receiving solid food (teaching). In essence, this is the believer who is walking in dependence upon the Spirit of God and by whom the Spirit of God is producing the life of Christ in him or her as manifested by his or her fruit. Like (*psuchikos*) earlier, the suffix "ikos" is added to the root word πνεῦμα (*pneuma*), and thus it communicates that the πνεῦμα (*pneuma*) is the dominating factor in this person's life. In contrast to the natural man who is governed by the human nature (*psuche*) in thought, word and deed, this person is governed by the Spirit (*pneuma*) of God in thought, word, and deed.

At this point in the exegesis, both sides of the carnal Christian debate would probably align. However, when verse one in chapter three is read, the two viewpoints become more divergent. The carnal man is the third category of man that Paul describes, and this is to whom Paul wrote this section of the letter. The word translated "carnal" in verse one is the Greek word σάρκινος (*sarkinos*), which literally means "fleshly, material, made or consisting of flesh."[120] This word is only used to describe one other person in Scripture: the apostle Paul himself! In Romans 7:14 Paul says, "For we know that the law is spiritual, but I am **carnal** (*sarkinos*), sold under sin." Interestingly enough, Paul uses a second Greek word translated *carnal* in verses three and four. That Greek word is σαρκικός (*sarkikos*), which means "fleshly, carnal, pertaining

---

[120] Zodhiates, <u>The Complete Word Study New Testament</u>, 1279-1280.

to the flesh or body."[121] In commenting on the relationship between the two words, the Theological Dictionary of the New Testament says, "It (σάρκινος) differs in no way from **σαρκικός**."[122] However, Dr. Ryrie sees a subtle difference in meaning: "Some see no difference in the meaning of the two words, but probably most do. If there is a difference, it is this: **Sarkinos** means 'made of flesh,' that is, weak but without attaching any blame to that condition…On the other hand, **sarkikos** does have an ethical or moral connotation. It means 'to be characterized by the flesh, something that is willful and blameworthy.' The first word means 'made of flesh,' while the second means 'controlled by the flesh.'"[123]

This begs the question: Who is Paul speaking to here? According to the lordship teachers quoted above, there is no such thing as a continuously "carnal" Christian, and this *category* of Christian is completely fabricated by modern theologians as an explanation of the worldliness found in churches today. However, Paul begins this section with a key indicator as to *whom* he is speaking to: brethren! In fact, Paul uses the Greek word **ἀδελφός** (*adelphos*), translated "brethren" or "brother," of the Corinthians in every chapter of this epistle, except for chapter thirteen (1:10; 2:1; 3:1; 4:6; 5:11; 6:5, 8; 7:29; 8:12-13; 9:5; 10:1; 11:2; 12:1; 14:6; 15:1; 16:15). This is a strong indication that Paul viewed these Corinthians as believers and yet still referred to them as carnal in this passage. It seems like exegetical gymnastics for MacArthur to claim, as he did above, that Christians can *behave* carnally, but that does not mean that they *are* carnal, especially when Paul himself says directly that the Corinthian believers *are* carnal!

Not only does Paul say that the Corinthians are carnal, but he says that they are "still" carnal in verse three. The word "still" ἔτι (*eti*) is an adverb modifying "carnal" and sets forth an ongoing condition that has persisted over some amount of time. Carnality among believers does not automatically resolve itself over time, and this is the case with these Corinthian Christians.[124] When Paul wrote 1 Corinthians, the believers were about five years old in the faith…"[125] Dr. Ryrie poses a good question at this point: "How long should

---

[121] Zodhiates, The Complete Word Study New Testament, 1279.
[122] Kittel, Bromiley, and Friedrich, Theological Dictionary of the New Testament, 144.
[123] Ryrie, So Great Salvation, 61.
[124] Rokser, "Examining Lordship Salvation Pt. 6."
[125] Ryrie, So Great Salvation, 63.

it take before a believer might be considered spiritual? The answer to this question would depend upon whom one asks. The lordship proponents would answer, "Not long." Even though they would be unable to identify or quantify that amount of time, they would still hold stringently to their answer. Consider the comments by John Piper: "Could it be that the reason you have not made any progress beyond those early days is that you really are no different than ordinary natural men? He doesn't want to believe it. And he doesn't treat them that way. He gives them the benefit of the doubt. But the warning is sounded! Not to make progress in Christian maturity is dangerous... But let's not treat continued immaturity as unimportant. It could be a sign that no true spiritual life was ever present and that the professing Christian is only a natural man after all."[126] In short answer to Piper's rhetorical question: "Yes, it is possible that someone who is living carnally is not really saved." It is true — just because someone thinks they are saved or says they are saved, it does not mean that they are saved.

However, what lordship teachers falsely assume is that one can know this for sure by someone's external, public life. However, the only thing one *can* determine by external, public acts is carnality, NOT whether or not someone is saved. When someone is manifesting the works of the flesh, as listed in Galatians 5:19-21, then they are clearly being governed by the sinful human nature, whether saved or unsaved. Thus, manifested sin in someone's life is never an accurate measurement of one's salvation. Salvation is based solely upon whether or not one has Jesus Christ as his or her substitute when it comes to the payment for the penalty of sin. When confronted with believers sinning *too much* (again, never quantified), lordship teachers always seem to revert back to their doctrine of temporal insecurity. If the full penalty for every "act of sin" was paid 2,000 years ago on the cross of Jesus Christ, then no "act of sin" is an issue, as it relates to the penalty of sin (i.e., hell). Acts of sin, however, are an issue in spiritual growth and practical sanctification because when believers are carnal (governed by the sinful human nature), they are not growing spiritually. Their salvation from the power of sin, which the Lord also wants to provide, is non-existent, and thus

---

[126] John Piper, "The Danger of Being Merely Human," *Desiring God*, Last Modified February 21, 1988, accessed March 16, 2012, http://www.desiringgod.org/resource-library/sermons/the-danger-of-being-merely-human.

they are out of fellowship with the Lord and unable to please Him or bear fruit.

In the following statement, Bing astutely points out the contradiction in the lordship teachers: "If lordship salvation is correct, the carnal Corinthian believers of 1 Corinthians 3 had broken their discipleship-salvation commitment. But neither lordship salvation nor the Scriptures posit how soon after one believes/commits he may break the commitment, or to what degree. This makes the lordship view of salvation subject to arbitrary standards to define conduct necessary for those who would be accepted as truly saved. It does not deal satisfactorily with the reality of sin in the believer's life and the process of growth and maturity."[127] Does the Bible allow for people making false professions? Absolutely! But, does the Bible also allow for carnal Christians? Absolutely! Is this the ideal state for a believer? Absolutely not!

In contrast to the lordship teachers' stance on the issue of carnal Christians, the Bible clearly states in 1 Corinthians 3 that believers can be carnal, and this state of carnality can be a continuing state, as exhibited by the Corinthian believers. However, this state is not ideal, nor should it be condoned, but it is indeed a reality that can be true of Christians. In this state, the believer is dominated, controlled, or ruled by his or her sinful nature to the extent that, when he or she is in this state, he or she is unable δύναμαι (*dunamai*) to receive the solid food of the Word of God. As a result, the believer, who is fully blessed with all spiritual blessings in the Heavenly places (Ephesians 1:3), who is filled up and complete in Christ (Colossians 2:10), and who has all he or she needs to live godly in this life (2 Peter 1:3-4) can actually live and walk like an unsaved person.

If the believer cannot live like an unsaved person, it makes all of Paul's exhortations/commands towards godly living and "putting off" the sinful deeds of the flesh irrelevant. Paul says that one of the outcomes of walking after the flesh, or living in a carnal state, is having one's understanding darkened and thus alienated from the life of God (see Ephesians 4:17-19). This would explain why a carnal Christian is unable to receive the Word of God: one has the capacity to, just as any believer does, however, when the believer is in a carnal state, he or she is unable to at that point in time. Why were the Corinthian believers not able to receive solid food in the past (*imperfect* tense used in 3:2b), and why were they still not able to receive solid

---

[127] Bing, Lordship Salvation, 162-163.

food currently (*perfect* tense used in 3:2c)? Paul answers, "For you are still carnal" (3:3a). The translated "still" is the Greek word ἔτι (*eti*) meaning "yet, or still," and it implies duration.[128] In other words, Paul is saying the Corinthian believers are carnal, even as he writes the letter. He addresses them as "brethren" in verse 1, and, two verses later, he addresses the same people (i.e., brethren) as being *still* carnal.

Additionally, Paul poses the question in Romans 6:1 that appears to be at the heart of this issue for the lordship teachers: "What shall we say then? Shall we continue in sin that grace may abound?" Here is Paul's chance to put this entire issue to rest, as he raises this question. Paul gives an answer that both sides of the argument should be able to say a hearty "Amen" to: God forbid or may it never be! What is Paul's reason for answering in such an emphatic way? Believers' relationship to sin has changed because believers have died to sin. This was Paul's chance to say what lordship teachers so clearly articulate, and, that is: "If one continues in sin, then this proves that one was *never* really saved because a truly saved person can never be *continuously* carnal." However, Paul does not give this answer, or even hint at this answer, because he focuses the believer on his or her co-crucifixion with Christ. He takes a positional stance, which emphasizes the believer's new identity in the Christ-accomplished work of Christ. Zuck clearly articulates the impracticalness of the lordship view on carnality when he states: "If one commits everything to Christ to be saved, where is there room for growth and development in the Christian life, as the Bible clearly encourages? And what happens if a believer falls into sin? The lordship gospel does not make allowance for carnality. Not that carnality is condoned or should go unchallenged. But it is seen in the Bible. To say that every believer consistently obeys the Lord overlooks examples of many believers in the Bible who lapsed into sin."[129]

In addition to this non-recognition of carnal believers, lordship teachers go to extreme lengths to state that believers cannot even be dominated by sin. For example, MacArthur says: "Though Christians do fall into sin from time to time, through their own disobedient choices, they are never again the slaves of sin as they were before being rescued by Christ and

---

[128] Zodhiates, The Complete Word Study New Testament, 2089.
[129] Zuck, "Cheap Grace?"

set free. Sin no longer has the power to control them."[130] MacArthur then quotes the fourth-century Church father John Chrysostom, who says: "How is it that sin can reign in you? It is not from any power of its own but only from your laziness."[131] The ironic thing about this quote is that it actually implies that sin can reign in the believer through one's own laziness or lack of diligence in understanding the truth that the sin nature *does not have to reign over* him or her. Thus, Chrysostom was not saying that sin reigning over the believer is impossible, but rather that it was possible, just not preferable. However, this is not what MacArthur teaches. In fact, he states in his commentary on Romans: "The idea that a Christian can continue to live habitually in sin not only is unbiblical but irrational. Christians obviously are able to commit many of the sins they committed before salvation, but they are not able to live perpetually in those sins as they did before…It is not merely that Christians *should not* continue to live in the realm and dimension of sin but that they *cannot*."[132] MacArthur says that sin **_cannot_** reign over the believer while the free grace side would say that sin **_should not_** reign over the believer, but that it still **_can_**. There is a huge difference between the two emphases. One (lordship) says that it is physically impossible for sin to reign over a believer, and the other (free grace) says that it is possible but not desirable. However, what does the Scripture say?

In the later part of Romans chapter six, Paul clearly teaches that sin can *still* reign in the believer's life. He states: "Therefore do not let sin reign in your mortal body, that you should obey it in its lust." The word *reign* is the Greek word βασιλεύω (**_basileuo_**), meaning to reign, to rule, and to have predominance. This is the typical word used to describe the reign of kings, and it is used of the King of Kings Himself in Revelation 11:15. In Romans 6:12, βασιλεύω (**_basileuo_**) is used in the present tense, which indicates that the ability of sin to reign in the believer's life is a "right now," continuing (or daily) possibility. It emphasizes the truth that a believer must actively rely upon the truth of one's death with Christ to sin, as a source of influence in one's life.

---

[130] MacArthur, Slave, 202.

[131] MacArthur, Slave, 203.

[132] John MacArthur, Jr., The MacArthur New Testament Commentary: Romans 1-8, (Chicago: Moody, 1991), 317.

If Paul must command the believer <u>NOT</u> to do something, this clearly implies that it can happen! Thus, for Paul to tell the believers not to let sin reign in their mortal bodies implies that they can let sin reign in their mortal bodies. Otherwise, Paul's use of the imperative carries no weight and would have been better expressed by an indicative mood (a statement of fact). In fact, this is the contrast we see between what Paul writes in the Scriptures, and what the lordship camp teaches. Paul commands believers not to let sin reign in their mortal bodies, implying that they can obey or disobey that command (i.e., an imperative); whereas, lordship teachers simply teach that believers cannot or will not let sin reign in their mortal bodies (i.e., an indicative). If this truth were indeed a statement of fact (i.e., indicative) as lordship teachers communicate, then there would be no need for an imperative in this area – it would just happen naturally!

Following verse twelve in Romans six, Paul says this: "And do not present your members *as* instruments of unrighteousness to sin, but present yourselves to God as being alive from the dead and your members *as* instruments of righteousness to God." The word *present* is the Greek word παρίστημι (*paristemi*) meaning to place, to stand, or to set something or someone before.[133] This word is also used in the present tense, which indicates that the believer has the ability to "right now" and *continually* present his or her members as instruments of unrighteousness to sin. As mentioned in chapter two, this negated command has the idea, *Stop continuing*.[134] Thus, Paul's charge to the believers in Rome could be two-fold: (1) Stop continuing to allow oneself to be dominated by the sin nature through the presentation of one's members, or (2) From this moment forward, stop presenting one's members to the sin nature because one will be dominated by it. Most likely, both of these emphases can be found in Paul's exhortations.

Clearly, Paul is making the point that believers can not only "fall into sin from time to time," as MacArthur admits, but they can also continually be in a state in which they present their members as instruments of unrighteousness. This is a real possibility for believers. Romans 6:16 sums it up well: "Do you not know that to whom you present yourselves slaves to obey, you are that one's slaves whom you obey, whether of sin *leading* to death, or of obedience *leading* to righteousness?" It is ironic that MacArthur wrote an

---

[133] Zodhiates, <u>The Complete Word Study New Testament</u>, 3936.
[134] Wallace, <u>Greek Grammar Beyond the Basics</u>, 724.

entire book on the meaning of this word, "slave," using it as his title. The Greek word is δοῦλος (*doulos*) meaning "one who is in a permanent relation of servitude to another, his will being altogether consumed in the will of the other."[135] It reflects someone who is bound to serve. Verse sixteen communicates that the believer has the possibility of being a slave to two separate entities: (1) sin, leading to death, or (2) righteousness (i.e., the Lord). Notice, too, that Paul uses the present tense indicative for the word translated "are" in the phrase — "you are that one's slave whom you obey." Thus, one is "right now" either the slave of sin or the slave of righteousness, depending upon whom one is presenting one's members to by faith. This seems to clearly describe a continually carnal Christian who is dominated by the sin nature.

In fact, when one considers the body of imperatives that Paul uses in his writings, regarding this area of the believer not living in carnality and not being dominated by sin, one sees that it is quite staggering. Consider the following non-exhaustive list: **Romans**: 6:11 (*reckon*), 6:12 (*reign*), 6:13 (*present*), 6:19 (*present*), 12:2 (*conformed* and *transformed*), 12:21 (*overcome*), 13:14 (*put on* and *make*); **1 Corinthians**: 4:16 (*imitate*), 6:18 (*flee*), 6:20 (*glorify*), 7:2 (*have*), 7:3 (*due*), 7:5 (*deprive*), 7:9 (*marry*), 10:7 (*become*), 10:10 (*complain*), 10:14 (*flee*), 10:31 (*do*), 11:1 (*imitate*), 15:33 (*deceived*), 15:34 (*awake* and *sin*) 15:58 (*be*); **2 Corinthians:** 6:14 (*be*), 6:17 (*out* and *separate* and *touch*), 8:24 (*show*), 13:5 (*examine* and *test*); **Galatians:** 5:13 (*serve*), 5:16 (*walk*), 6:1 (*restore*), 6:7 (*deceived*); **Ephesians:** 4:25 (*speak*), 4:26 (*angry* and *sin* and *go*), 4:27 (*give*), 4:28 (*steal* and *labor*), 4:29 (*proceed*), 4:30 (*grieve*), 4:31 (*put away*), 4:32 (*be*), 5:1 (*be*), 5:2 (*walk*), 5:3 (*named*), 5:7 (*be*), 5:8 (*walk*), 5:11 (*fellowship* and *expose*), 5:15 (*see*), 5:17 (*be*), 5:18 (*drunk* and *filled*), 5:22 (*submit*), 5:25 (*love*), 5:33 (*love*), 6:1 (*obey*), 6:2 (*honor*), 6:4 (*provoke* and *bring*), 6:5 (*obedient*), 6:9 (*do*), 6:10 (*strong*), 6:11 (*put on*), 6:13 (*take up*), 6:14 (*stand*), 6:17 (*take*); **Philippians:** 1:27 (*conduct*), 2:12 (*work*), 4:1 (*stand*), 4:6 (*anxious*), 4:8 (*meditate*), 4:9 (*do*); **Colossians:** 2:6 (*walk*), 3:1 (*seek*), 3:2 (*set your mind*), 3:5 (*put to death*), 3:8 (*put off*), 3:9 (*lie*), 3:12 (*put on*), 3:15 (*rule*), 3:16 (*dwell*), 3:18 (*submit*), 3:19 (*love*), 3:20 (*obey*), 3:21 (*provoke*), 3:22 (*obey*), 4:1 (*give*); **1 Thessalonians:** 5:13 (*peace*), 5:14 (*warn*), 5:15 (*see* and *pursue*), 5:16 (*rejoice*), 5:17 (*pray*), 5:18 (*give*), 5:19 (*do no quench*), 5:21 (*hold fast*), 5:22 (*abstain*); **2 Thessalonians:** 2:15 (*stand fast* and *hold*); **1 Timothy:** 4:7 (*reject* and *exercise*), 4:11 (*command* and *teach*), 4:12 (*be*), 4:15 (*meditate* and *give*), 4:16 (*take* and *continue*), 4:22 (*share* and *keep*), 6:2 (*do not despise* and *serve*), 6:5 (*withdraw*), 6:11 (*flee* and *pursue*), 6:12 (*fight* and *lay hold*);

[135] Zodhiates, The Complete Word Study New Testament, 1401.

2 Timothy: 1:13 (*hold fast*), 2:15 (*diligent*), 2:16 (*shun*), 2:19 (*depart*) 2:22 (*flee* and *pursue*), 3:14 (*continue*), 4:5 (*watchful*); **Titus:** 3:9 (*avoid*), 3:14 (*learn*). "Commands to obey become irrelevant and illogical if obedience is assured. Either the New Testament honestly exhorts believers to obedient Christian living, understanding the real possibility of failure, or the strong ethical sections of the Apostles' writings are reduced to logical absurdities."[136] Because of its emphasis in Paul's writings, it is clear that believers can be carnal (fleshly); otherwise, he would not have addressed it with so much consistency!

Another area that lordship teachers are very unclear on in is the area of justification and sanctification, and how they relate with one another. Consider the following quotes by lordship teachers:

Do not separate justification and sanctification so radically that you allow for one without the other. This is the error of *antinomianism*. God will not justify those He does not sanctify. God does not offer justification as a stand-alone means of salvation. Election, regeneration, faith, justification, sanctification, and even glorification are all integral facets of God's saving work... Justification cannot be isolated and made to represent the sum of God's saving work. Yet that is exactly the error that is rampant in contemporary theology.[137]

Sanctification, we believe, is inseparable from justification. Justification refers to the very salvation event whereas sanctification refers to the process of spiritual development. And we believe that justification and sanctification are inseparable so those who were truly justified are being sanctified. Those who experienced the saving event are in spiritual progress and it shows up in their life.[138]

While justification and sanctification are distinct theological concepts, both are essential elements of salvation. God will not declare a person righteous without also making him righteous. Salvation includes *all* God's work on our behalf from His foreknowledge of us before the foundation of the world to our ultimate glorification in eternity future (Romans 8:29-30). One cannot pick and choose, accepting eternal life while rejecting holiness and obedience. When God justifies an individual, He also sanctifies him.[139]

---

[136] Butcher, "A Critique of *The Gospel According to Jesus*."
[137] MacArthur, The Gospel According to Jesus, 197.
[138] MacArthur, "A Prayer for Complete Sanctification."
[139] MacArthur, The Gospel According to Jesus, 187.

Before dealing with the whole of the aforementioned quotes, it is too tempting to pass up mentioning that "sanctification" is conspicuously absent from Romans 8:29-30 — the very verse MacArthur quotes to support his teaching on experiential sanctification and how it naturally and logically follows justification. Pastor Dennis Rokser comments on this error in lordship salvation: "Yet it is noteworthy that sanctification is conspicuous by its absence between the believer's justification and glorification. Why? I am convinced that it is because while justification and glorification are guaranteed by God for every believer, it is not guaranteed (though desired and provided by God and His grace) for every believer to experience ongoing progressive sanctification."[140] As it will be shown with great clarity, God does indeed guarantee positional sanctification based on the work of Christ for the believer who has put his or her faith in Christ and His work. It is the progressive aspect, or experiential sanctification, that is not guaranteed but that is abundantly provided.

Another lordship teacher who comments on this area of sanctification and justification extensively is John Piper. In his printed sermon entitled *Slaves to God, Sanctification, Eternal Life*, he says, "So the big purpose of Romans 6 is to show why justification by faith *always* brings sanctification with it…Without this deliverance from the rule and slavery of sin – without a new direction of righteousness and holiness in our lives – we will not inherit eternal life… the result of being freed from sin and being enslaved to God and then bearing the fruit unto sanctification is eternal life. These steps are *not optional*. This is the only path that leads to eternal life: being freed from the slavery to sin, enslaved to God, bearing fruit in a life of holiness, and finally eternal life. That is why holiness and the fight against sin in this chapter is so serious. We are not playing games. *Eternal life is in the balance*."[141] (*italics mine*) Piper concludes his article with this statement: "So justification is necessary for eternal life as the legal ground or basis of it, which we obtain by faith; and sanctification, is necessary for eternal life as the public evidence that our faith is real."[142]

---

[140] Dennis Rokser, "Examining Lordship Salvation Pt. 8," *Grace Family Journal* Vol. 12, No. 58 Summer (2009).

[141] John Piper, "Slaves to God, Sanctification, Eternal Life," Desiring God, Last modified December 10, 2000, accessed February 10, 2012, http://www.desiringgod.org/resource-library/sermons/slaves-to-god-sanctification-eternal-life.

[142] Piper, "Slaves to God."

In the area of progressive sanctification, the lordship terminology becomes the most confusing. While they[143] define sanctification as having three components (positional, experiential, and ultimate), they focus more on the experiential component of sanctification due to their faulty gospel. The "proof" that one is truly believing and committed (surrendered) is whether one is exhibiting experiential sanctification. For example, John MacArthur's defines experiential sanctification this way: "And that's where we live, folks, right now… (this one) fluctuates."[144] He further describes this experiential sanctification as the following: "We are in this process period between past sanctification and future sanctification, being sanctified which is the *decreasing frequency and incidents of sin and increasing holiness*" (italics added).[145] The question can rightfully be asked, "Who gets to define *decreasing frequency of sin* and *increasing holiness?*" According to Piper quoted above: "We are not playing games. *Eternal life is in the balance*… sanctification, is necessary for eternal life as the public evidence that our faith is real." The nebulousness of the lordship teaching is astounding when one considers that, on one hand, it decries the seriousness of not living a holy life (resulting in eternal damnation), and yet, on the other hand, it makes "exceptions" to the type of perfection or non-perfection that God will accept in their experiential sanctification process. Incredibly, lordship teachers cannot define their terms biblically (such as *decreasing frequency of sin* and *increasing holiness*), so they provide little to no clarity on the doctrine of sanctification. Thus, like many other areas, lordship teachers speak out of both sides of their mouths.

Regarding the different aspects of sanctification, the Bible speaks with great clarity. Charles Ryrie distinguishes these different aspects of sanctification in his book *So Great Salvation*. He says: "Even of the carnal Christians at Corinth Paul dared to say that they were washed, they were sanctified, and they were justified (1 Corinthians 6:11). The same tense (indicating an accomplished fact, not something to be attained) is used for all three verbs. This aspect of sanctification separates all believers to their new position as belonging to God… *Positional sanctification* is an actual position that is not dependent on the state of one's spiritual growth and maturity…But quite obviously all believers do not evidence this position in their practices.

---

[143] MacArthur, "A Prayer for Complete Sanctification."
[144] MacArthur, "A Prayer for Complete Sanctification."
[145] MacArthur, "A Prayer for Complete Sanctification."

Sanctification therefore has a second aspect (*Experiential sanctification*) which relates to the progressive work of continuing to be set apart during one's entire Christian life. Every biblical exhortation to godly living underscores this aspect of sanctification (1 Peter 1:16)" (italics added).[146]

In addition to 1 Corinthians 6:11, some additional verses that utilize the <u>aorist</u> tense, thereby emphasizing the positional point in time aspect of sanctification, are: *John 17:17*, "**Sanctify** them by Your truth. Your word is truth"; *1 Thessalonians 5:23*, "Now may the God of peace Himself **sanctify** you completely; and may your whole spirit, soul, and body be preserved blameless at the coming of our Lord Jesus Christ"; *Hebrews 13:12*, "Therefore Jesus also, that He **might sanctify** the people with His own blood, suffered outside the gate." Other verses that utilize the <u>perfect</u> tense, which emphasizes the past completed work of sanctification (i.e. positional sanctification) with its results continuing in the present are: *Acts 20:32*, "So now, brethren, I commend you to God and to the word of His grace, which is able to build you up and give you an inheritance among all those who **are sanctified**,"; *Acts 26:18*, "To open their eyes, *in order* to turn *them* from darkness to light, and *from* the power of Satan to God, that they may receive forgiveness of sins and an inheritance among those who **are sanctified** by faith in Me,'"; Romans 15:16, "That I might be a minister of Jesus Christ to the Gentiles, ministering the gospel of God, that the offering of the Gentiles might be acceptable, **sanctified** by the Holy Spirit,"; *1 Corinthians 1:2*, "To the church of God which is at Corinth, to those who **are sanctified** in Christ Jesus, called *to be* saints, with all who in every place call on the name of Jesus Christ our Lord, both theirs and ours"; *Hebrews 10:10*, "By that will we **have been sanctified** through the offering of the body of Jesus Christ once *for all*"; and *Jude 1*, "Jude, a bondservant of Jesus Christ, and brother of James, To those who are called, **sanctified** by God the Father, and preserved in Jesus Christ."

Bob Wilkin, President of the Grace Evangelical Society, wrote in his article *We Believe In: Sanctification—Part 2: Past Sanctification* the following:

When most authors or speakers write or speak about *sanctification,* they almost always *mean progressive* (or *present*) *sanctification*. In fact, many of the books and articles on sanctification never even *mention* past sanctification. One wonders why there is such a neglect of the subject of past sanctification. It is not because the Scriptures are silent on the subject. One

---

[146] Ryrie, <u>So Great Salvation</u>, 150-151.

might well think that the reason for this lack of attention is because many *more* passages speak of present sanctification than speak of past (or future) sanctification. Before embarking on this study, I thought that way. However, after doing a study of all New Testament passages dealing with sanctification, I found that over three quarters deal with past sanctification! By comparison only 20% deal with present sanctification.[147][148]

This is an insightful observation, which should at the minimum, be reflected in one's teaching of the subject. However, when one observes lordship teaching, one would think the exact opposite were true – that over 75% of the sanctification passages deal with experiential/daily sanctification and only 20% deal with past or positional sanctification. The exact *opposite* emphasis should be alarming! Why is the biblical emphasis and that of the lordship teachers so different?

The answer is that lordship teachers miss the impact of this completed past positional aspect of sanctification even though their definition of

---

[147] Bob Wilkin, "We Believe in Sanctification Part 2: Past Sanctification," Journal of the Grace Evangelical Society on Faith Alone, Last modified Spring 1993, accessed April 2, 2012 - Volume 6:10, http://www.faithalone.org/journal/1993i/Wilkin.htm.

[148] Wilkin, "We Believe in Sanctification." **Appendix I: NT Passages Dealing with Past, Present, and Future Sanctification (Total = 117):** Past Sanctification (90 Passages, 76.9%), Present Sanctification (24 Passages, 20.5%), and Future Sanctification (3 Passages, 2.6%). **Appendix 2: Passages Dealing with Present Sanctification (Total=24):** John 17:17, 19 (both *hagiazo*), Rom 6:19 (*hagiasmos*), 1 Cor 7:34 (*hagios*), 2 Cor 7:1 (*hagiosyne*), 1 Thess 3:13 (*hagiosyne*); 4:3, 7 (both *hagiasmos*); 5:23 (*hagiazo*), 1 Tim 2:15 (*hagiasmos*); 4:12; 5:2 (both *hagneia*), 22 (*hagnos*), 2 Tim 2:21 (*hagiazo*), Titus 2:5 (*hagnos*), Heb 12:10 (*hagiotes*), James 4:8 (*hagnizo*), 1 Pet 1:15, 16; 3:5 (all *hagios*), 1 John 3:3 (*hagnizo*), Rev 22:11 (*hagios* and *hagiazo*). **Appendix 3: Passages Dealing with Past Sanctification (Total=90):** I. Pre-Conversion Sanctification (Total = 5): I Cor 7:14 (*hagiazo* [twice] and *hagios*), 2 Thess 2:13 (*hagiasinos*), I Pet 1:2 (*hagiasmos*). **II. Forensic Sanctification (Total = 13):** 1 Cor 1:30; 6:11 (both *hagiazo*), Col 3:12 (*hagios*), Heb2:11 (*hagiazo* [twice]); 3:1 (*hagios*); 10:10, 14, 29; 13:12 (all *hagiazo*), 1 Pet 1:22 (*hagnizo*), 2 Pet 1:21 (*hagios*), Rev 20:6 (*hagios*). III. Intrinsic Sanctification (Total = 5): Rom 6:6 (concept), 22 (*hagiasmos*), Eph 5:26 (*hagiazo*), Heb 9:14 (*katharizo*), Rev 22:11 (*hagios* and *hagiazo*). IV. Positional Sanctification (Total = 67): A. Passages Using *Hagiazo* (Total = 3) Acts 20:32; 26:18, Jude l; B. Passages Using *Hagios* (Total = 64), Acts 9:13, 32, 41; 26:20, Rom 1:7; 8:27; 12:13; 15:25, 26, 31; 16:2, 15, 1 Cor 1:2 (twice); 6:1,2; 14:33; 16:1, 15, 2 Cor 1:1; 8:4; 9:1, 12; 13:13, Eph 1:1,4, 15, 18; 2:19; 3:8, 18; 4:12; 5:3; 6:18, Phil 1:1; 4:21,22, Col 1:2,4, 12,26, 1 Thess 3:13; 5:27 (in the Majority Text), 2Thess 1:10, I Tim 5:10, 2 Tim 1:9, Phlm5,7, Heb 6:10; 13:24, Jude 3, 14, Rev 5:8; 8:3,4; 11:18; 13:7, 10; 14:12; 15:3; 16:6; 17:6; 18:24; 19:8; 20:9

sanctification incorporates it. For example, Piper states: "Morever, justification is **_an event_** that happens at **_a point in time_**, and is not an **_ongoing act_** of God as sanctification is" (italics added).[149] This statement in and of itself is a true statement; however, because of the lordship gospel, lordship teachers do not emphasize the positional aspect of sanctification after their initial definition. After they define the positional aspect of sanctification, they never mention it again. This would be akin to a family who is excited for their annual trip, which they look forward to all year. They load the family vehicle, the children's toys, videos, and electronic devices. Then, as they pull out of the driveway to head out on the trip, they leave one of their kids at home. From the definition stage to the practical teaching stage, positional sanctification is not "brought along for the ride." This is confusing to the highest degree, as it leads one to wonder, "Who indeed has been sanctified, and who is being sanctified?" Pastor Dennis Rokser comments, "...while Lordship Salvation teachers give lip service to a distinction between justification before God and progressive sanctification in time, their homogenizing of these two wonderful truths has led to a garbling of the Gospel, confusion about the condition for salvation, an annihilation of absolute personal assurance of eternal life, a failure to distinguish the believer's position in Christ which is perfect and his practice which is far from perfect, and a myriad of other problems contrary to the Scriptures."[150] Wilkin correctly, but sadly states, "No level of progressive sanctification is guaranteed in this life to the person who has experienced past sanctification. Great growth in holiness is possible. So, too, little growth—or even a decrease in holiness! — is a sad possibility. Believers must be diligent in order for progressive sanctification to be experienced to the fullest degree."[151]

Because the lordship teacher's arguments are so confusing, especially regarding their _guaranteed_ doctrine of progressive sanctification, many questions arise. **Question #1: If progressive/experiential sanctification is guaranteed, why do Christians not progress according to the same spiritual growth rate?** Everyone's walk with the Lord is different and unique in relationship to one's growth, exposure to solid teaching of truth,

---

[149] Piper, Future Grace, 402.

[150] Dennis Rokser, "Examining Lordship Salvation, Pt. 7," _Grace Family Journal_ Vol. 12, No. 57 Spring (2009).

[151] Wilkin, "We Believe in Sanctification."

understanding of truth, responsiveness to truth, etc. If progressive/experiential sanctification were indeed guaranteed by God, one should see **everyone** progressing at the same rate, according to the same schedule, but clearly one does not see this. Biblical examples clearly reveal that people grow at different rates. First, there is Martha and Mary — Mary is clearly more advanced in her understanding and response to the presence of Jesus (Luke 10:38-42). Second, there is Peter and the other Disciples — Peter is clearly responding more to revelation from the Father than the other disciples are when it comes to Jesus' true identity (Matthew 16:13-17). Third, there is Paul and Peter/Barnabas — Paul had a much clearer understanding of the gospel of grace (and that the Mosaic Law had no part in justifying or sanctifying believers) than Peter and Barnabas when it came to eating with the Gentiles (Galatians 2:11-16). Fourth, there is Paul and Barnabas concerning John Mark — The contention was so sharp between Paul and Barnabas in regard to bringing John Mark along with them on their second missionary journey that they split up (Acts 15:36-41). However, years later, not only had John Mark become effective in ministry, but he was then profitable to the apostle Paul (2 Timothy 4:11).

    <u>Question #2: If progressive/experiential sanctification is guaranteed, why do there appear to be different levels of reward at the judgment seat of Christ?</u> Even though lordship teachers say (like free grace teachers do) that not every believer will walk away from the judgment seat of Christ with the same level of reward, their teaching contradicts this. According to their teaching, the same level of reward would be guaranteed if in fact progressive/experiential sanctification were guaranteed. MacArthur inadvertently reveals this contradiction when he writes the following in his book *Slave*: "On the other hand, those believers who spend their lives in temporal and worthless pursuits should expect minimal reward from Christ. The sins of every believer are, of course, forever forgiven through the Cross; salvation cannot be forfeited. Yet those who squander their God-given opportunities for spiritual service will one day discover that their works consist of little more than wood, hay, and stubble. Lacking any eternal value, such works will not stand up under the fire of God's scrutiny (1 Corinthians 3:12-15)."[152]

---

[152] MacArthur, <u>Slave</u>, 184.

1 Corinthians 3:11-15 clearly teaches the concept of varying reward based upon varying degrees of faithfulness in believers. The foundation of Jesus Christ is said to be laid for ***every*** believer, and there is no other foundation that can be laid (verse 11). Still, it is clear that believers can build upon this foundation with different materials such as gold, silver, precious stones, wood, hay, and/or straw (verse 12). Thus, not every believer builds with the same materials. Believers will have different and varying levels of faithfulness throughout their lives. They will do some good works via improper motives or through the strength of the flesh. Hence, believers can and will do some things, even apparent "good" things, in a way that God will deem unacceptable to Him, due to the source from which they do it. Why is this so? Although every believer has been positionally sanctified and has been given everything needed for a godly life (2 Peter 1:3-4), they can walk according to the flesh. This clearly contradicts lordship teachers' "guaranteed" stance in relation to progressive/experiential sanctification.

Another passage that clearly contradicts the lordship teaching of guaranteed progressive/experiential sanctification is 2 Corinthians 5:9-10. This passage explains that the believer's aim is to be well pleasing to the Lord (verse 9). Why is this the case? According to Paul in verse 10, all will appear before the judgment seat of Christ. Once one is there, it is clear that one will receive reward based on what he or she did while in his or her physical body. To assume that progressive/experiential sanctification is guaranteed would negate the need for Jesus Christ to delineate what was good (acceptable) or bad (unacceptable) because everyone would then be at the same level, and hence all would then be rewarded the same. Clearly, this will not be the case. In this passage, Paul is exhorting the Corinthian believers to live faithfully, which is well pleasing to the Lord. Thus, the mere fact that Paul exhorts the Corinthian believers to live faithfully shows they can live unfaithfully to the Lord.

Lordship teachers lead one to believe that God guarantees progressive/experiential sanctification in much the same way that He will guarantee it during the Millennial Kingdom. In Jeremiah 31:31-34, Jeremiah describes the New Covenant as a "new" covenant with the house of Israel and the house of Judah (not the Church). He says this in verses 33-34: "But this *is* the covenant that I will make with the house of Israel after those days, says the LORD: I will put My law in their minds, and write it on their hearts; and I will be their God, and they shall be My people. No more shall every man teach his neighbor, and every man his brother, saying, 'Know the LORD,' *__for__* *__they all shall know Me__*, from the least of them to the greatest of them, says the LORD. For I will forgive their iniquity, and their sin I will remember no more." (***emphasis mine***). Hence, during the New Covenant made with the house of Israel and Judah, no one will need a teacher, and everyone will have the same level of knowledge and same closeness to the Lord. Constable comments: "All Israelites, from the least to the greatest, would also know the Lord intimately, without having to be exhorted to do so."[153] This "group inclusion phenomenon" is only promised here to the house of Israel and Judah. Nothing like this is repeated or taught in the Church age, contrary to the lordship teaching of guaranteed progressive/experiential sanctification.

For lordship teachers to have the same definition of the term "sanctification," as free grace teachers do is mind-blowing when considering the vastly different outcomes that both sides reach. According to lordship teachers, progressive sanctification must follow salvation. Without progressive "proof" of the Christian's life becoming more like Christ, lordship teachers conclude that the Christian must not have surrendered or committed his or her life to the lordship of Christ, and, hence was never really saved. Lordship teachers clearly ignore clear biblical terms (i.e. *carnal* Christian) and discard them as unbiblical. They explain away clear biblical concepts such as *reward, different growth rates, different levels of fruit bearing*, etc. Lordship teachers sadly promote their false gospel by any means necessary, even if it means using creative and misleading hermeneutics. As Paul rightly says, "A little leaven leavens the whole lump" (Galatians 5:9).

---

[153] Thomas L. Constable, "Notes on Jeremiah," *Plano Bible Chapel*, last modified 2019, accessed November 23, 2019, https://www.planobiblechapel.org/tcon/notes/html/ot/jeremiah/jeremiah.htm.

CHAPTER 4
Legalism: Working to Maintain Salvation

Legalism is an eight-letter word that carries with it the full impact of the proverbial "four letter" word in our society. Whichever way the word is defined, nobody wants to be a legalist! Zane Hodges agrees when he states, "No one wants to be accused of it (being called a legalist) any more than one would want to be accused of despising motherhood or apple pie. In ecclesiastical circles, to call someone a legalist is to hurl an insult of the first magnitude."[154] Realizing many claim that lordship salvation promotes legalism, it would be wise to define legalism to validate and prove this claim. Although lordship teachers are purportedly anti-legalism by their own admission, it will be shown that lordship teachers do in fact, encourage legalism in the Christian life, even if they do not admit this.

A free grace advocate, Fred Chay, a former pastor and currently a Professor of Theology and Dean of Doctoral Studies at the Grace School of Theology and the Managing Editor of Grace Theology Press, defines legalism this way:

Legalism is keeping man-made rules and regulations in order to earn God's acceptance for salvation or sanctification...Legalism is a term Evangelical Christians use to describe a certain doctrinal position or practice that emphasizes a system of rules and regulations in achieving either salvation or spiritual growth...Legalism is any man-made system, set of rules, mandated expectations, or regulations that promise that God will give acceptance and approval in return for, or as a reward for, human effort and obedience.[155]

---

[154] Zane Hodges, "Legalism: The Real Thing," *Journal of the Grace Evangelical Society,* Volume 9:17 (Autumn 1996): accessed June 30, 2012, http://www.faithalone.org/journal/1996ii/Hodges.html.

[155] Fred Chay, "Legalism is Lethal in the Spiritual Life," Grace Line Ministry, accessed June 30, 2012, http://www.graceline.net/Articles/Legalism%20is%20Lethal%20in%20the%20Spiritual%20Life.pdf,.

Moreover, Pastor Dennis Rokser from Duluth Bible Church, another Free Grace proponent, states, "I have defined legalism in my teaching as the false belief that justification before God or progressive sanctification in time can be obtained by religious works or rituals."[156]

Interestingly enough, lordship teachers would define legalism similarly. For example, John MacArthur gives this description of legalism:

Legalism believes that every act, every habit, every type of behavior is either black or white. Legalists live by rules rather than by the Spirit. They classify everything as good or bad, whether the Bible mentions it or not. They develop exhaustive lists of do's and don'ts. Doing the things on the good list or avoiding the things on the bad list is their idea of spirituality, no matter what the inner person is like. Their lives are law-controlled, not Spirit-controlled. But refraining from doing things is not spiritually walking in the Spirit.[157]

Moreover, John Piper describes legalism with the following two components: "(1) Treating biblical standards of conduct as regulations to be kept by our own power in order to earn God's favor, and (2) The erecting of specific requirements of conduct beyond the teaching of Scripture and making adherence to them the means by which a person is qualified for full participation in the local family of God, the church."[158]

Thus, just like in sanctification, the lordship definition of legalism is right in line with the free grace definition. In fact, lordship proponents seem to despise legalism as much as the free grace proponents. What then is the issue? Just as with sanctification, having the right definition, does not always guarantee right theology is practically taught. Interestingly enough, it is a statement from Piper's very own definition, which sheds light on the fact that is subtly missed in many discussions of legalism. Many people can agree that erecting additional requirements, beyond the teaching of Scripture, to live the Christian life or please God is legalism. However, even using "biblical standards" (i.e., the Law) is also an improper way to please God and earn His

---

[156] Dennis Rokser, "A Critique of Zane Hodges' Article – 'The Hydra's Other Head: Theological Legalism'," *Grace Family Journal* **Vol. 11, No. 54 Special Edition** (2008).

[157] John MacArthur, Jr., The MacArthur New Testament Commentary: 1 Corinthians, (Chicago: Moody, 1984), 189.

[158] John Piper, "Flesh Tank and Peashooter Regulations," *Desiring God*, last modified January 17, 1982, accessed July 2, 2012, http://www.desiringgod.org/resource-library/sermons/flesh-tank-and-peashooter-regulations.

favor and this is rarely discussed as a form of legalism. A complete definition of legalism should be defined as the following: the use of any law (man-made or God-given) in an attempt to either gain justification and/or sanctification and/or to earn God's favor in general.

Both free grace and lordship teachers agree that legalism is dangerous. In fact, when comparing legalism to licentious sins, such as alcoholism, Piper even says this: "Legalism is a more dangerous disease than alcoholism because it doesn't look like one. Alcoholism makes men fail; legalism helps them succeed in the world. Alcoholism makes men depend on the bottle; legalism makes them self-sufficient, depending on no one. Alcoholism destroys moral resolve; legalism gives it strength. Alcoholics don't feel welcome in church; legalists love to hear their morality extolled in church."[159] Moreover, Charles Swindoll in his book *The Grace Awakening* says this when describing the danger of legalism, ""Killers cannot be mildly or kindly tolerated. You can no more allow legalism to continue than you could permit a rattlesnake to slip into your house and hide. Before long somebody is going to get hurt"[160]

The bottom line is that legalism is deceptive, ultimately undefinable, and continually takes the focus off the finished work of Christ as the basis of one's acceptance before God and puts the focus back on oneself for one's acceptance before God. It is this moving set of standards, this vagueness, which allows legalism to fit so well with lordship salvation (like a hand in a glove). Unfortunately, it is this same reason that both lordship salvation and legalism are extremely dangerous and deceptive because they look "holy," sound "holy," and appear to be a "harder and tougher" standard of righteousness. Because legalism is a moving set of undefinable standards, which are not clearly delineated in the Scriptures, it fits perfectly with Lordship's undefinable level of commitment, surrender, lack of habitual sinning, etc. that has already been discussed. The question – "How much is really enough?" – is a great question, as are the questions – "How often?", "How consistently?", and "What constitutes when something is not enough?"

The better question is "What do the Scriptures say?" When it comes to law keeping for justification or sanctification, the Bible is very clear. In fact, James 2:10 states, "For whoever shall keep the whole law, and yet stumble in one *point,* he is guilty of all." Moreover, Paul says the following to those trying

---

[159] Piper, "Flesh Tank and Peashooter Regulations."
[160] Swindoll, Grace Awakening, 98.

to keep the Law for their justification and/or sanctification in Galatians 5:3: "And I testify again to every man who becomes circumcised that he is a debtor to keep the whole law." Both of these verses delineate very clear standards for someone who wants to keep the Law. On the negative side, James says that you can be perfect in keeping the entire Law, and, yet, if you stumble in one point, you are guilty of breaking all the Law. On the positive side, Paul says that if you take up one component of the Law, you are indebted to keep the whole thing. There is no picking and choosing when it comes to the Law; it is either keeping all 613 commandments contained therein or following none of them.

In contrast to the clear teaching of Scripture, notice how vague lordship teachers are when speaking of law-keeping. For example, MacArthur states, "The law is still important to the Christian. For the first time, he is able to meet the law's demands for righteousness (which was God's desire when He gave it in the first place), because he has a new nature and God's own Holy Spirit to empower his obedience."[161] Furthermore, MacArthur states in his book *The Gospel According to Jesus*, "Implicit obedience to His commandments is the necessary, expected, and natural fruit of genuine love for Him. It is also therefore the telltale mark of authentic saving faith."[162] In his book *Following Christ* R.C. Sproul agrees with MacArthur when he states, "Unless the believer's sanctification is evidenced by true conformity to the commandments of Christ, it is certain that no authentic justification ever really took place…Christ is a commandment-giving Lord. If one has true justifying faith, he moves diligently to pursue the righteousness of obedience that Christ demands."[163]

So, now, "perfect" law-keeping is not only within the believer's grasp, but, according to MacArthur and Sproul, it is the necessary, expected, and natural fruit of authentic saving faith. MacArthur and Sproul readily admit that they themselves are not perfect in keeping the Law, nor are any believers perfect. However, this puts them and their theology in a quandary because, according to God's Word, His standard is perfection and not just a "willingness to obey,"[164] as lordship proponents convey. For instance,

---

[161] MacArthur, The MacArthur New Testament Commentary: Romans 1-8, 364.
[162] MacArthur, The Gospel According to Jesus, 32.
[163] Sproul, Following Christ, 329.
[164] MacArthur, The Gospel According to Jesus, 99.

MacArthur states in his book *Hard to Believe*, "Obedience is the key word. The only visible evidence you will ever have of your salvation is a life lived *in the direction* of obedience; it is the proof that you genuinely have bowed to the lordship of Jesus Christ and been transformed by His grace into a servant of His righteousness." (*italics added for emphasis*)[165]

By reducing the standard of perfection to a "willingness to obey" or a "life lived in the direction of obedience," the lordship camp is actually softening the requirements set forth by God Almighty in relationship to His Law. As supposed proponents of God's Law, with the free grace camp labeled "antinomian," the lordship group actually dishonors God with a man-made, man-accepted, worldly approach to the Law. Their approach amounts to just "trying your hardest" to "do the best you can." This is a slap in the face to God's standard of perfection. God does not grade "on the curve," as lordship teachers seem to imply. In fact, James 2:10 requires perfection in all points of the Law, or, if not, that person is guilty of breaking all of it. Based upon the perfect standard of the Word of God, and matching it up with MacArthur's teaching regarding the Law (i.e., needing to obey it to prove authentic faith), nobody would or could produce the necessary "telltale mark of authentic saving faith." In other words, nobody can be saved because nobody can keep the Law perfectly and thereby prove his or her less than authentic conversion. This is a salvation based upon works and not upon grace. Grace requires nothing because it is unmerited favor based upon God's work for us.

If law keeping is promoted in the Christian life, then oftentimes it is promoted for justification as well. Paul recognized this in Galatia when he wrote the epistle to the Galatians. The faulty teaching in the Christian life gradually worked its way backward into a false justification message. Additionally, once the false teaching regarding law keeping worked its way back into the justification message, it naturally advanced further in Christian life teaching. Paul's question to the Galatians in 3:3 grabs one's attention as one considers this issue today: "Are you so foolish? Having begun in the Spirit, are you now being made perfect by the flesh?" This is exactly what lordship salvation has done in its teaching. Because lordship teachers reduce the requirements of the Law to merely a "willingness to obey," they have created a sanctification that is not clearly defined. This trickles back to their justification message, which also includes a nebulous "willing to submit" as a

---

[165] MacArthur, <u>Hard to Believe</u>, 112-113.

prerequisite for justification. Macarthur in a sermon entitled "Fundamental Christian Attitudes: Obedience," says the following about justification: "God's part: I save you, I forgive your sins, I give you eternal life through the work of Jesus Christ. Your part: you repent and you submit to follow Me. That's salvation. When you came to salvation, that's what you did – that's what you did, you committed to obedience, though you didn't fully understand all the implications involved in that."[166]

In regard to legalism in justification and sanctification it is important to understand Colossians 2:6. Colossians 2:6 says, "As you therefore have received Christ Jesus the Lord, so walk in Him." Paul uses the word "as" to describe a comparison and similarity between justification (i.e., "as you therefore **have received** Christ Jesus the Lord") and sanctification ("so **walk** in Him"). It would make sense that if one were confused as to how to "receive" Christ Jesus the Lord that one would be confused as to how to "walk in Him." Legalism in justification will always manifest itself in legalism in sanctification, and vice versa. The two clearly go hand-in-hand. This is why it is so important to note that one receives Christ Jesus the Lord by faith in His finished work alone (John 1:12). Thus, the believer is to walk by faith in the finished work of Jesus Christ alone. In justification, the believer is to rely upon (at a moment in time) the finished work of Jesus Christ for deliverance from the penalty of sin. This work is where Christ died FOR individuals' sins and rose again the third day. In sanctification, the believer is to rely upon (moment by moment) the finished work of Christ for deliverance from the power of sin. This work is where individuals died WITH Christ to sin and were raised WITH Christ to newness of life.

Another vague quote, regarding obedience, comes from MacArthur's book *Slave* in which he says, "Once again the obedient slave has nothing to fear from facing the Master. As R.C.H. Lenski observed, 'He who, as a slave to Christ, submits his will to him *in all he does* is well pleasing to God and need never fear to stand before his judgment seat.'" (*italics added for emphasis*)[167] MacArthur's implication is that if one does not submit his or her will to God in *all he or she does*, one does indeed have something to fear before God's

[166] John MacArthur, "Fundamental Christian Attitudes: Obedience," *Grace To You*, last modified September 22, 1996, accessed December 6, 2019, https://www.gty.org/library/sermons-library/90-115/fundamental-christian-attitudes-obedience.
[167] MacArthur, Slave, 184.

judgment seat. However, what disciple has ever lived this type of perfect life? *All* is a pretty inclusive word! The following quote from MacArthur is just as dogmatic when it comes to progressive sanctification: "That is perfect sanctification, to *always* do exactly what God does, to *always* do exactly what God wills, to *always* do exactly what God tells you to do. That is perfect sanctification, to *always* do the will of God. In John 6:38 we follow the same thought, 'I have come down from heaven, not to do My own will, but the will of Him who sent Me.' He is the model of what sanctification is. Sanctification is *always obeying* the will of God."[168]

The words "all" and "always" make it an "all or nothing" proposal, and thus the lordship view is clear: perfect sanctification is the standard by which one can ascertain whether or not he or she is truly saved. However, realizing that this is an untenable extreme, lordship teachers further "muddy the waters" by speaking out of both sides of their mouths. For example, in MacArthur's *The Gospel According to Jesus*, he states, "A moment of failure does not invalidate a disciple's credentials."[169] Free grace advocate, Dr. Charles Ryrie comments on MacArthur's quote when he states:

"My immediate reaction to such a statement is to want to ask if two moments would? Or a week of defection, or a month, or a year? Or two? How serious a failure and for how long before we must conclude that such a person was in fact not saved? Lordship teaching recognizes that 'no one will obey perfectly,' but the crucial question is simply how imperfectly can one obey and yet be sure that he 'believed' in the lordship/mastery sense? If 'salvation requires total transformation' and I do not meet that requirement, then am I not saved? Or if my transformation is less than total at any stage of my Christian life, was I not saved in the first place?"[170]

MacArthur gave another confusing comment in a sermon in which he compared how Israel was saved with how individuals in the Church age are saved. He said:

And at that part, at that point when you were receiving all of that from Him, you were responding by saying, 'Yes, Lord, and I will follow

---

[168] John MacArthur, "The Power of Scripture in the Process of Sanctification," *Grace to You*, last modified March 20, 2005, accessed February 11, 2012, http://www.gty.org/resources/sermons/90-287/the-power-of-scripture-in-the-process-of-sanctification.

[169] MacArthur, The Gospel According to Jesus, 199.

[170] Ryrie, So Great Salvation, 48.

You.' And that was the covenant of salvation. 'I confess you as Lord,' and Lord means the one in charge, and that's what you confessed. And at that point, in God's eyes, the blood that had been splattered on Christ, the sacrifice, was then splattered on you, because of your part in the covenant. It's a beautiful picture. So when you came to salvation, my friend, you made a simple covenant of obedience. The sad story of Israel is that they did – what – they violated it. And so do we – and so do we. If there's anything that has to be the companion of faith, it must be obedience, because those two were the companions when we were saved, right? Faith in the Savior as the only one to save us; commitment to obey the Lord as our King.[171]

In this statement, MacArthur shares how sad it is that Israel violated their covenant with God by their disobedience. This is true, but what happened to them as a result? He seems to imply that they, therefore, were not saved, but he does not state this explicitly. Then in his quote, MacArthur goes on to say, "and so do we – and so do we." What is he implying here? He seems to indicate there must be a certain level of obedience to secure salvation.

The ongoing confusion and vagueness communicated by lordship teachers is in many ways due to the fact that they do not recognize the believer's proper relationship to the Law. In an effort to support their commitment/surrender salvation, they impose the Law upon the believer as a rule of life. Unfortunately, the *Westminster Confession of Faith* agrees with them and states, "Although true believers be not under the law as a covenant of works, to be thereby justified or condemned; yet it is of great use to them…as a rule of life (Chapter XIX, Section VI)." Consider also Dr. Martin Lloyd-Jones, a well-known Reformed theologian who states, "The Christian must never say farewell to the law. Thank God, we are no longer under it as a way of salvation; but we are to keep it, we are to honor it, we are to practice it in our daily life."[172] Additionally, another well-known Reformed theologian, J.C. Ryle states, "Genuine sanctification will show itself in habitual respect for God's law, and habitual effort to live in obedience to it as a rule of life. The

---

[171] MacArthur, "Fundamental Christian Attitudes: Obedience."

[172] David Martyn Lloyd Jones, <u>Romans: Exposition of Chapter 7:1-8:4; The Law: Its Functions and Limits,</u> (Edinburgh, UK: Banner of Truth, 1973), 27.

Holy Spirit…will always lead him (the believer) to a spiritual use of the law in the pursuit of sanctification."[173]

However, is the law really the rule of life for the Church-age believer's life? Is this what the Scripture teaches? Zane Hodges disagrees adamantly with the lordship teachers and states, "The Mosaic law perceived as a rule of life for believers – whether or not that has soteriological overtones – is *true legalism!*"[174] When considering the Law of God, one must consider its original purpose and original audience. When God delivered His people Israel out of slavery in Egypt through the hand of His servant Moses, He took them into the wilderness. Before God gave them the Promised Land, He first gave them the Law that would govern their lives in the Promised Land. The Law as an entire unit was comprised of 613 laws, which governed and regulated not only their spiritual lives but also their ceremonial lives and their civil lives. However, contrary to popular belief, Jewish thought does not allow for this Law to be broken apart and taken as many different individual pieces. It was either all 613 laws or none of it. As Alva McClain, founder and first president of Grace Theological Seminary, wrote, "This law is one law – an indivisible unity. While it is unquestionably true that at least three elements – moral, ceremonial, and civil – appear within this law, it is wrong to divide it into three laws…or, as is popularly done, divide it into two laws, moral and ceremonial."[175] Godet adds, "In general, the distinction between the ritual and moral elements of the law is foreign to the Jewish conscience, which takes the law as a divine unity."[176] Moreover, with only one exception,[177] the word "law" is always found in the singular in the New Testament, invariably emphasizing the divine unity of the Law.

What then is the purpose of the Mosaic Law, as clearly defined in the New Testament? Former pastor and author Ron Merryman describes five clearly defined purposes for the Law in the New Testament. They include the following:

---

[173] Miles J. Stanford, The Complete Green Letters, (Grand Rapids: Zondervan, 1975), 263.
[174] Hodges, "Legalism: The Real Thing."
[175] Alva J. McClain, Law and Grace: A Study of New Testament Concepts as They Relate to the Christian Life, (Winona Lake, IN: BMH Books, 1954), 8.
[176] Frederic L. Godet, Commentary on St. Paul's Epistle to the Romans, (New York: Funk and Wagnalls, 1892), 144.
[177] A quotation from the Septuagint of Jeremiah 31:33 in Hebrews 8:10 & 10:16 the word "law" in the New Testament is always found in the singular.

(1) The Law was given to stop every mouth - that is, to muzzle every voice that would flaunt self-righteousness before God. Merryman cites Romans 3:19, which says, "Now we know that whatever the law says, it says to those who are under the law, *that every mouth may be stopped*, and all the world may become guilty before God."

(2) The Law was given to produce in every human being a sense of personal guilt, accountability, and hence a need for God's forgiveness. Merryman cites Romans 3:19 again with an emphasis on the last phrase: "*and all the world may become guilty before God,*"

(3) The Law was given to provide an objective knowledge of sin for the human race. Merryman cites Romans 3:20, which states, "Therefore by the deeds of the law no flesh will be justified in His sight, *for by the law is the knowledge of sin,*"

(4) The Law was given to serve as a stern child disciplinarian to bring its hearers to Christ that they might be declared righteous by God through faith in Christ's finished work on the cross. Merryman cites Galatians 3:24, which says, "Therefore *the law was our tutor to bring us to Christ*, that we might be justified by faith,"

(5) The Law was given to serve as a restrainer of evil and a perpetual reminder to unbelievers of their moral responsibility to God. The Law is categorically not made for the believer. Merryman cites 1 Timothy 1:8-10, which states, "But we know that the law *is* good if one uses it lawfully, knowing this: that the law is not made for a righteous person, but for *the* lawless and insubordinate, for *the* ungodly and for sinners, for *the* unholy and profane, for murderers of fathers and murderers of mothers, for manslayers, for fornicators, for sodomites, for kidnappers, for liars, for perjurers, and if there is any other thing that is contrary to sound doctrine."[178]

Noticeably absent from this list is the verse that describes how the believer must keep the Law in order to grow in holiness, or to be progressively sanctified. This is because this verse does not exist nor is this teaching found anywhere in Scripture. In fact, verses that dictate the exact opposite are found multiple times, but the clearest of these expressions is found in Romans 6:14, which says, "For sin shall not have dominion over you, for you are not under law but under grace." In fact, the book of Romans is a clear road map for the

---

[178] Ron Merryman, The Believer and the Mosaic Law: Growth Truth for Believers, (Casa Grande, AZ: Merryman Ministries, 2002), 3-10.

Christian life. Romans 1-5 describes how one is saved from the penalty of sin or the doctrine of justification. Romans 6-8 describes how one is saved from the power of sin in daily life, and how one is saved from the very presence of sin in the future (the doctrines of sanctification and glorification). Romans 9-11 deals with God's plans for the nation of Israel and describes His distinct purpose for them. Romans 12-16 finishes the book with practical instruction involving daily life for the believer in Jesus Christ.

It is interesting to note that the teachers who place the believer under the law for the Christian life tend to view Romans 6-8 from a justification perspective rather than a sanctification perspective. In fact, MacArthur, in giving his own outline of the book of Romans, says:

"Remember the context of all of this. The major theme of Romans is justification by faith. In other words, you're saved not by keeping the law but by believing, right? Through grace. Now we have started with justification by faith in chapter 3, the first couple of chapters showed us how sinful we are...we hit chapter 3 verse 21 and we get into justification by faith and it runs all the way to the end of chapter 8. Chapter 3, 4, 5, 6, 7, and 8...all justification by faith, that's the theme of all of those. And then in 9 to 11 he applies it to Israel and then in 12 till the end he shows how it works out in living."[179]

Thus, in essence, lordship teachers communicate that one is not justified by keeping the Law, but they imply that the believer in Jesus Christ IS under the law for sanctification.[180] Piper also thinks that being "under Law" only refers to justification and of the righteousness needed to enter Heaven. In a printed sermon titled *What is the Meaning of "Under Law" and "Under Grace"?—Part 1*, Piper says this about Romans 6:14:

"So from all this I conclude that being 'under law' means that law-keeping is the way we will provide a righteousness that lets us stand before God. If we treat the law in such a way that law-keeping provides the righteousness that justifies us, then we are 'under law.' But being 'under grace' means that we receive as a free gift all our righteousness, namely, the righteousness of Christ, by grace as the ground of our justification. That is the gift. That is the basis of our right standing with God. Christ was born and

---

[179] John MacArthur, "Dead to the Law," *Grace to You*, last modified February 13, 1983, accessed August 10, 2012, http://www.gty.org/resources/sermons/45-50/dead-to-the-law.

[180] R.C. Sproul, "From Slaves of Sin to Slaves of God," *Ligonier Ministries*, accessed August 8, 2012 http://www.ligonier.org/learn/sermons/slaves-sin-slaves-god/.

lived under law and fulfilled it perfectly by faith. That is His righteousness. We escape from being 'under law' by trusting Christ as our righteousness. That is what it means to be under grace." [181]

MacArthur adds:

What does he (Paul) mean (in Romans 6:14), that you don't have to do anything anymore? Do you not have to live a moral life or obey God? No! What he means is that you are no longer under the power of the penalty of the law. It can't kill you anymore; you can only die once. That's all, only once. Christ died on the Cross, and you, by faith, died in Him. That pays the penalty, so in that sense, you are no longer under the law. That is, the law has no power to slay you. The law had a penalty, the wages of sin is death, and Christ took the penalty. [182]

Moreover, MacArthur states:

Therefore, to be "under the law" in Paul's terminology is to be *under the law as a means of justification*. It is crucial to understand the way the apostle Paul uses this expression. When he says we are not under the law but under grace in Romans 6, he is not discarding the *moral teachings* of the law. He is not lending credence to any sort of antinomian doctrine. He is not minimizing the sin of disobedience to the moral teachings of the law…Paul's consistent teaching with regard to the law is that it can never be a means of justification. And when he says we are 'not under law,' he means we do not ground our justification in our own personal obedience. We are no longer trying to justify ourselves by obedience to the law. [183]

The irony of this statement is that MacArthur does teach that obedience, or a willingness to obey, is a requirement of true saving faith. If he

[181] John Piper, "Free From Sin, Slaves of Righteousness, Part 1," *Desiring God*, last modified November 26, 2000, accessed July 17, 2012, http://www.desiringgod.org/resource-library/sermons/free-from-sin-slaves-of-righteousness-part-1.

[182] John MacArthur, "Christ and the Law, Part 3," *Grace to You*, last modified March 4, 1979, accessed July 28, 2012, http://www.gty.org/resources/sermons/2211/christ-and-the-law-part-3.

[183] John MacArthur, "How Does Grace Free us From the Law," *Pyromaniacs: Setting the World on Fire*, last modified June 14, 2010, accessed July 28, 2012, http://teampyro.blogspot.com/2010/06/hoe-does-grace-free-us-from-law.html.

is not talking about obedience to the law of God, what type of obedience is he speaking of?[184]

Biblically, what the lordship teachers communicate, regarding the Law's ineptitude to justify a man before God, is true. However, their use of Romans 6:14 to prove this point is a faulty interpretation. In fact, their interpretation for Romans 6:14 could not be farther from the truth and farther from the context of the passage. The first five chapters of Romans dealt over and over again with this very issue (i.e. justification). Romans 3:21-22 says, "But now the righteousness of God apart from the law is revealed, being witnessed by the Law and the Prophets, even the righteousness of God, through faith in Jesus Christ, to all and on all who believe. For there is no difference." Moreover, Romans 3:28 says, "Therefore we conclude that a man is justified by faith apart from the deeds of the law." Furthermore, Romans 4:16 says, "Therefore it is of faith that it might be according to grace, so that the promise might be sure to all the seed, not only to those who are of the law, but also to those who are of the faith of Abraham, who is the father of us all."

Romans 6 is not dealing with the unbeliever's deliverance from the penalty of sin (i.e., justification) through the death of Jesus Christ on the cross for the unbeliever, but rather it is dealing with the believer's deliverance from sin's power (i.e., sanctification) through one's own co-crucifixion and co-resurrection with Christ. Everything is in place in order for the believer to walk victoriously over the power of sin in his or her daily life through one's co-crucifixion and co-resurrection with Christ. The "key" to walking in righteousness is to reckon or count oneself to have died to sin and to be alive to God in Christ Jesus the Lord. From this reckoning, one can then present his or her members as instruments of righteousness to God. Paul communicates this reckoning further in Romans 7 when he clearly states that believers have died to the Law with Christ in order to be made holy. Thus, if

---

[184] As shared in an earlier chapter, in his book <u>The Gospel According to Jesus</u>, MacArthur states on page 122, "Salvation is by grace through faith. It has nothing to do with meritorious human works. But the only possible response to God's grace is a broken humility that causes the sinner to turn from his old life to Christ. The evidence of such a turning is the willingness to submit and *obey*. If coldhearted *disobedience* and deliberate rebellion continue unabated, there is good reason to doubt the reality of a person's faith."

this is the case, then what does the phrase "under law" mean in Romans 6:14 if it is not talking about justification?

In his booklet *What is the Believer's Rule of Life?*, Pastor George Zeller states, "It is clear from Romans 6:14 that Paul is talking about being free from sin's dominion and power and authority, which is what sanctification is all about."[185] Sanctification deals with deliverance from sin's dominion on a daily basis; whereas, justification deals with sin's penalty. If Romans 6:14 and the phrase "under law" refers to justification, then Paul would have discussed sin's penalty and NOT sin's dominion or power. Thus, this verse not only teaches a believer's deliverance from the Law, but it also clearly demonstrates sin's dominion over an individual that seeks to walk by a law system.[186] Notice the condition for sin to not have dominion over a believer – "for you are not under law but under grace." Thus, it is implied that if the believer lives according to the Law, then sin WILL have dominion over them.

The Greek preposition ὑπό (*hupo*), meaning under or beneath, is used in Romans 6:14 of both law and grace. It is talking about two different spheres – much like a rainy day when one transfers his or her place of standing from being under one umbrella to another umbrella. It is implied that a person can only be under one umbrella at a time. Merryman comments more on what the phrase "under the law" means when he says, "To be *delivered from the law*, to be *dead to the law*, *not to be under the law* means that the believer is freed from the condemnation of the Law and separated from it as a mode of operation. The Law is not a means of spiritual success; it is, in fact, just the opposite."[187] These are facts that are true of every believer, and God wants each believer to know that he or she no longer has to live in bondage to sin in his or her life. The reason for this is that a believer is not under law but under grace. Titus 2:11-12 teaches that it is the grace of God, not the Law of God, that teaches one to deny ungodliness and worldly lusts and teaches one how to live soberly, righteously, and godly in this present age. William Newell says it this way: "The believer is not under law, not under external enactments, not under conditions; but he has already an eternal standing in grace, - that is, in already secured Divine favor, by a sovereign act of God; which has not only reckoned

---

[185] George Zeller, <u>What is the Believer's Rule of Life? Is the Believer Under the Law as a Means of Sanctification?</u>, (Middletown, CT: Middletown Bible Church, 1999), 10.

[186] Merryman, <u>The Believer and the Mosaic Law: Growth Truth for Believers</u>, 15.

[187] Merryman, <u>The Believer and the Mosaic Law: Growth Truth for Believers</u>, 15.

to him Christ's atoning work, but has placed him fully in the place of Christ's present acceptance with God!"[188] Lordship teachers, with their legalistic teaching for sanctification, greatly reduce the beauty of one's full acceptance with God on the basis of Christ's work on one's behalf. Even more, they hold up individuals' commitment or surrender in justification as a test and their obedience to the Law in sanctification as another test as to determine whether or not they are truly saved or accepted by God. This is **NOT** grace! Grace by definition is unmerited favor, which means individuals cannot earn it or forfeit it by anything that they do or by anything that they do not do!

Thus, how do lordship teachers continue to view the Law as necessary for the Christian life? The reason they interpret Romans 6:14 through a justification lens is because the Law, in their teaching, holds a very special place in believers' sanctification. Even more, according to these men, they think that believers are now equipped, through the Holy Spirit, to keep the Law! For example, MacArthur says, "Because He (Jesus) fulfilled the whole law, so can you and so can I. That's the most amazing part of all. Because He was perfectly righteous, because He fulfilled all righteousness, you and I can too…You say, 'Could I ever fulfill the moral law?' The Bible says that if we walk in the Spirit, we will fulfill the righteousness of the law, because Christ in us fulfills it. What a climax! He fulfilled the law, and He fulfills it in us."[189] Elsewhere, MacArthur also states, "The law is still important to the Christian. For the first time, he is able to meet the law's demands for righteousness (which was God's desire when He gave it in the first place) because he has a new nature and God's own Holy Spirit to empower his obedience."[190] Moreover, Reverend Crenshaw states, "The law is God's commandments and shows us what God requires but is unable to produce the requisite righteousness; the Gospel gives legal righteousness in justification as a free gift, and consequently sanctifying righteousness is produced in us by the Spirit, enabling us to perform the law, though not perfectly in this life…The Reformed do not believe that keeping the law brings sanctification but that sanctification enables the believer to keep the law."[191] Crenshaw says later,

---

[188] William R. Newell, <u>Romans Verse by Verse</u>, (Chicago: Moody Press, 1938), 168.

[189] John MacArthur, "Christ and the Law, Part 1," *Grace to You*, last modified February 18, 1979, accessed July 28, 2012, http://www.gty.org/resources/sermons/2209/christ-and-the-law-part-1.

[190] MacArthur, Jr., <u>The MacArthur New Testament Commentary: Romans 1-8</u>, 364.

[191] Crenshaw, <u>Lordship Salvation: The Only Kind There Is!</u>, 154.

"Perfect holiness entails perfect law-keeping. The law is not a legal requirement to merit salvation or the power for sanctification but the path over which sanctification leads us."[192]

Since lordship proponents teach that the believer's sanctification is guaranteed, and that the Holy Spirit Himself enables the believer to keep the Law of God then why do true believers not keep the Law perfectly in this life? Furthermore, because God's standard for lawbreakers (found in James 2:10) is perfection (not messing up on even one component of the Law), can anybody truly be sanctified based on the guaranteed sanctification that lordship teachers reveal? Moreover, since sanctification cannot be separated from justification (as the lordship proponents teach), and since nobody can truly be sanctified, can anybody actually be justified according to their teachings? Also, if justification is directly tied to sanctification, should spiritual growth not happen at the same rate for each believer? Why not, if it is guaranteed as the lordship teachers promote? Furthermore, if the Law is holy and perfect (and it is), and the Holy Spirit is holy and perfect (and He is), why is the combination of the two unable to cause perfect sanctification in the believer's life (i.e., perfect obedience to the Law of God)?

It is clear from this line of questioning that lordship teachers are "backed into a corner" and either need to change their previously made comments or need to create a diversion to take the focus off their contradictory message. If one cannot keep the Law perfectly, even with the enabling power of the Holy Spirit, then lordship advocates must find fault with one of two participants: the believer or the Holy Spirit. Obviously, they would not put the blame on the perfect Holy Spirit of God, so it must be the believer's fault. Hence, they contradict themselves because now the believer's carnality is blamed, yet earlier the lordship teachers repudiate the possibility that a believer could be carnal. Lordship teachers cannot have it both ways! This is a glaring inconsistency in their interpretation. Moreover, although they claim to value and honor the Law of God, they change the Law's standard (perfection) to meet their own theology of sanctification, which is "the Holy Spirit helps us keep the Law *most of the time*, or a believer cannot keep the Law *perfectly in this life*."

This is the whole point of Paul's statement in Romans 6:14 - the believer's holiness of life, practical sanctification, cannot be taken up on the

---

[192] Crenshaw, Lordship Salvation: The Only Kind There Is!, 155.

basis of Law. The Law requires perfection, and, once a believer has broken the Law, he or she is no longer perfect. Additionally, according to Romans 6:14, if a believer is focused on keeping the Law, indwelling sin will have dominion over him or her. How can trying to keep the perfect, holy, and righteous Law of God actually contribute to being enslaved to indwelling sin? Romans 7 addresses this very issue and also reveals why the believer **cannot** and **must not** seek to grow spiritually by keeping the Law.

Any human effort for deliverance from sin is contrary to God's grace system and always leads to frustration.[193] This is why, in Romans 7, Paul does an incredible job, under the inspiration of the Holy Spirit, of explaining the believer's relationship to the Law. Additionally, he gives a personal example of what life will look like when the believer is trying to make him or herself holy by keeping the Law. Paul essentially gives his readers a real-life illustration of the truth of Romans 6:14 — that if one wants to live under Law, he or she will be dominated and ruled by indwelling sin.

What is the believer's relationship to the Law? Romans 6:14 communicates that the believer is "not under Law." This concept is further explained in Romans 7 through the use of a practical illustration. Romans 7:1-3 describes the law of marriage in this way: "Or do you not know, brethren (for I speak to those who know the law), that the law has dominion over a man as long as he lives? For the woman who has a husband is bound by the law to *her* husband as long as he lives. But if the husband dies, she is released from the law of *her* husband. So then if, while *her* husband lives, she marries another man, she will be called an adulteress; but if her husband dies, she is free from that law, so that she is no adulteress, though she has married another man." This is a very clear illustration and statement of fact that, according to the law of marriage, a person cannot exit a marriage unless there is a death to the other party. This arrangement was especially true in a Jewish marriage where the Mosaic Law did not permit a woman to divorce her husband. In fact, the illustration is so clear that most every lordship author would agree with the interpretation of the natural use of the law of marriage.

In Romans 7:4, Paul switches gears in mid-illustration. One expects Paul to say that the husband is the one who dies, and so the wife can then marry another husband, but that is not what he says. He tells us that the wife died, and now because of her death, she is free to marry another. Regarding

---

[193] Merryman, The Believer and the Mosaic Law: Growth Truth for Believers, 18.

this point, Watchman Nee writes, "How can I marry a second husband, if my first husband resolutely refuses to die? There is only one way out. If HE will not die, I can die, and if I die the marriage relationship is dissolved. And that is exactly God's way of deliverance from the Law. The most important point to note in this section of Romans 7 is the transition from verse 3 to verse 4. Verses 1 to 3 show that the husband should die, but in verse 4 we see that in fact it is the woman who dies. The Law does not pass away, but I pass away, and by death I am freed from the Law."[194] Now, that should cause the casual observer to exclaim, "Wait a minute! How can someone who died be able to still marry another? Once you are dead, you are DEAD, right?" George Zeller of Middletown Bible Church poses this very same question and rightly states, "But if I am dead, how can I be married to another? In Christ's death I died and in Christ's resurrection I LIVE! Thus, I can be joined in marriage to Christ!"[195] The only possible way this can happen is if the wife is raised from the dead with Christ. This is the beautiful and precious truth that Paul shares, starting in Romans 5:12 and continuing through chapter 8 — the believer has been identified with Christ in His death to sin and in His resurrection to newness of life.

Romans 7:4 reads, "Therefore, my brethren, you also have become dead to the law through the body of Christ, that you may be married to another — to Him who was raised from the dead, that we should bear fruit to God." This new relationship to the Law is one of the keys to living a fruit-bearing life to God. Paul uses the second person plural form of θανατόω (*thanatoo*) meaning "to put to death"[196] in this verse. In addition, this verb is an aorist, passive, indicative, which indicates that the corporate death experienced by all believers (i.e., my brethren) occurred at a point in time in the past, and the death was perpetrated on them. In other words, they did not kill themselves, but somebody put believers to death through the body of Christ. This somebody was none other than God Himself. Moreover, Romans tells us for what purpose God changed the believers' relationship to the Law when it says, "that you may be married to another...*that we should bear*

---

[194] Watchman Nee, The Normal Christian Life, (Wheaton, IL.: Tyndale, 1977), 161-162.

[195] George Zeller, "Romans Chapter 7: The Believer's Relationship to the Law," *Middletown Bible Church*, accessed August 10, 2012, http://www.middletownbiblechurch.org/romans/romans7.htm.

[196] Zodhiates, The Complete Word Study Dictionary: New Testament, 2289.

fruit to God." In conjunction with what one knows from other Bible passages, such as Ephesians 2:10 and John 15, God's purpose for the believer is to "bear fruit" (John 15:2), "more fruit" (John 15:2), and eventually "much fruit" (John 15:5). Implied in this act is that when believers still maintain their relationship to the Law as their rule of life, they will remain unfruitful. There is something unique about believers' new relationship — their new marriage — to the risen Christ that enables them to bear fruit unto God. This point cannot be underemphasized – the very thing that lordship teachers promote as their guide or rule of a "successful" Christian life is the very thing that: (1) Keeps believers in bondage to sin (Romans 6:14) and (2) Causes believers to remain unfruitful in their lives.

The lordship advocates twist Romans 7 to promote a legalistic Christian life teaching, which is a direct outflow of their commitment/surrender gospel. For instance, MacArthur states the following regarding believers' relationship to the Law, "So somebody asks the question: if we're free from the law as Christians, is the law binding on us? The answer is no and yes. It is not binding in the sense that our acceptance with God depends on it, it is binding in the sense that our new life seeks to serve it."[197] Could anything be more confusing than this statement? The answer is "no and yes!" Really? The Apostle Paul goes out of his way to use a common, every day, understandable example of the law of marriage to illustrate believers' change of relationship to the law, and yet MacArthur teaches that the law is binding on believers. Imagine if one were to carry MacArthur's teaching on believers' relationship to the Law into a physical example of marriage. If he did so, one could then be married to two people (i.e. the Law and Christ), which violates the very law of marriage!

John Piper adds another dimension to this discussion that also contradicts Paul's statements. Piper states:

What then shall we, as Christians, do with the holy, just and good law of God? Answer: we will look into this law for two purposes: 1) We will look into the law to see Christ so that we can know him and trust him and love him more. 2) We will look into this law to test ourselves to see if we do know and trust and love Christ as we ought. God's law reveals Christ in many ways, and we may use it to know him and stir up our love for him.

---

[197] MacArthur, "Dead to the Law."

And the law is a litmus paper to test the genuineness of our love to Christ.[198]

Thus, Piper encourages believers to look to their previous husband (i.e., the Law) to test whether or not they truly love their current spouse (i.e., Christ).

This again is clearly not what Paul was referring to in Romans 7. The reason believers have been put to death to the Law is so they can then function within the sphere of a productive marriage to the risen Christ rather than a destructive marriage to the Law, which is even referred to elsewhere as the "ministry of death" (2 Corinthians 3:7) and the "ministry of condemnation" (2 Corinthians 3:9). Ron Merryman says this about 2 Corinthians 3:7-9: "By divine design, the Moral Law produces death and condemnation, NOT LIFE AND RIGHTEOUSNESS. Do not expect the Ten Commandments (or moral Law) to stimulate your sanctification experience. They are very effective in pointing out your shortcomings and failures and creating a sense of condemnation, but they simply cannot produce life and growth."[199] Moreover, George Zeller of Middletown Bible Church states, "The law is a terrible husband -- strict, inflexible, stern, rigid, demanding and unbending. The Lord is a wonderful husband -- merciful, gracious, and He, by His power and life, ENABLES me to please Him. Just as a marriage relationship produces FRUIT (children), so my marriage to Christ produces fruit."[200]

MacArthur clearly distorts the phrase in Romans 7:4, which says: "that we should bear fruit to God." For instance, MacArthur says, "And then the end of verse 4, great truth, 'In order that we should bring forth...what?...fruit unto God.' That's the purpose. Because of Christ we bear fruit. May I remind you that this is not a command; this is a statement of fact. It could read, 'in order that we bring forth fruit...we do.' There's no such thing as a no-fruit Christian. Salvation has a product. Because of a transformed life, we bear fruit unto God."[201] MacArthur claims that the verb καρποφορέω (*karpophoreo*) translated "bear fruit" is a statement of fact rather than a command. Although, He is correct in stating that this verb is not a Greek imperative (command), if

---

[198] John Piper, "Dead to the Law, Serving in the Spirit, Part 1," *Desiring God*, last modified January 28, 2001, accessed August 10, 2012, http://www.desiringgod.org/resource-library/sermons/dead-to-the-law-serving-in-the-spirit-part-1.

[199] Merryman, The Believer and the Mosaic Law: Growth Truth for Believers, 14.

[200] Zeller, "Romans Chapter 7: The Believer's Relationship to the Law."

[201] MacArthur, "Dead to the Law."

it were to be a statement of fact, it would be in the indicative mood. This verb is in the subjunctive mood. Daniel Wallace, Greek Scholar and Professor at Dallas Theological Seminary, defines the indicative mood, in his book *Greek Grammar Beyond the Basics*, by stating: "The indicative mood is, in general, the mood of assertion, or presentation of certainty."[202] Wallace distinguishes the subjunctive by stating: "The subjunctive can be said to represent the verbal action (or state) as uncertain but probable...it is better to call it the mood of probability..."[203] Moreover, William Mounce, former pastor and Director of the Greek program at Gordon-Conwell Theological Seminary, distinguishes and contrasts the indicative and subjunctive moods by stating: "As it is normally stated, the indicative is the mood of reality. It states what is...the subjunctive does not describe what is, but what may (or might) be. In other words, it is the mood not of reality but of possibility (or probability)."[204]

1. Referring back to Romans 7:4, is it possible for the believer to bear fruit to God? Yes, it is possible and probable, but, because the mood is not indicative but rather subjunctive, this fruit bearing is not a guaranteed statement of fact as described by MacArthur. Only a person with a bent theological bias (such as lordship or commitment salvation) could read this meaning into the text. This is rather disconcerting, as John MacArthur studies the Word of God and utilizes the biblical languages. Hence, one can conclude the following about his teaching on this topic: (1) He does not understand the difference between the Greek indicative and subjunctive moods, (2) He does not observe the mood in this particular verse, even though he apparently notices it is not an imperative, or (3) He knows it, but he chooses to emphasize what he wants to emphasize here (i.e., he has a theological bias that he is driving into this text). No matter which of these conclusions is correct, they are all fraught with concerns. As the subjunctive mood would seem to indicate in Romans 7:4, there is such a thing as a "carnal Christian," which was

---

[202] Wallace, Greek Grammar Beyond the Basics, 448.

[203] Wallace, Greek Grammar Beyond the Basics, 461.

[204] William D. Mounce, Basics of Biblical Greek, (Grand Rapids, MI: Zondervan Publishing House, 1993), 289.

discussed in previous chapters. Still, carnality is not the goal for the believer's life; rather, as Romans 7:4 teaches, the believer's goal is fruit bearing to the glory of God. This is because the believer has a new relationship to the Law (i.e., dead to it) and a new relationship to Christ (i.e., alive unto God and joined to Christ).

It is clear from Romans that believers will not/cannot bear fruit unto God if they are still trying to do so by relating to the Law. It is only as they learn to relate to their new spouse, in union with Him, that they bear fruit. John 15:5 says, "I am the vine, you *are* the branches. He who abides in Me, and I in him, bears much fruit; for without Me you can do nothing." Notice Jesus does not include keeping the Law as a necessary element in bearing fruit. In fact, in Romans 7:5, one sees that the sin nature is actually "aroused by the law" to bear fruit to death. It states, "For when we were in the flesh, the sinful passions which were aroused by the law were at work in our members to bear fruit to death." Unfortunately, MacArthur glosses over verse 5 as a description that was true of the believer before he or she became saved. MacArthur teaches that the believer can now take up the law as his or her rule of life. Moreover, MacArthur teaches that the believer no longer has a sin nature;[205] thus, he teaches that the "sinful passions" referred to here no longer exist in a believer's life. On the concept of indwelling sin, MacArthur writes the following:

…as both Scripture and experience clearly teach, the remaining humanness somehow retains certain weaknesses and propensities to sin. The tyranny and penalty of sin both in and over the Christian's life have been broken, but sin's potential for expression in his or her life has not yet been fully removed. One's human weaknesses and instincts make him or her capable of succumbing to Satan's temptations when he lives apart from the Spirit's Word and power.[206]

By MacArthur's definition, one's unredeemed human body is somehow the source of sin, and so the deliverance from one's human body will someday deliver him or her completely from his or her sin that is

---

[205] George Zeller, "John MacArthur's One Nature Position," *Middletown Bible Church*, accessed December 13, 2019,
   http://www.middletownbiblechurch.org/doctrine/1natjm01.htm.
[206] MacArthur, Jr., The MacArthur New Testament Commentary: Romans 1-8, 325-326.

somehow wired into the body. Is MacArthur not really just describing a "carnal Christian," who is susceptible to succumbing to sin from time to time? His own words continue to build on what appears to be a mountain of contradictions.

Contrary to John MacArthur's teaching, the apostle Paul gives a bone chilling description — a personal example of his own experience with his sin nature and his efforts of trying to keep the law. In Romans 7:13-24, Paul describes his agony of wanting to "do right" but not finding the strength to do so. Additionally, he describes the agony of not wanting to "do wrong" and yet not finding the strength to overcome the sinful desires of his flesh. This is exactly what Paul refers to in verse 5. The law arouses one's sin nature, which works in one's members and produces fruit unto death; hence, God prepared through Christ one's death to the Law, one's deliverance from the Law, and one's new relationship to Christ. It is interesting to note that the very thing lordship teachers try to produce (i.e., fruitful Christians) is the very thing they guarantee they will **NOT** produce through their law-based, legalistic sanctification teaching. They do not understand their new relationship to the risen Christ and the impact this new relationship has on their previous relationship to the Law. This separation (death) from the Law is actually key to living life from an entirely new source – as one alive from the dead in Christ, united with Him.

This lack of understanding is clearly denoted in the way that MacArthur and Piper both interpret this section in Romans 7. In verse 6, Paul writes, "But now we have been delivered from the law, having died to what we were held by, so that we should serve in the newness of the Spirit and not *in* the oldness of the letter." The Greek word translated "delivered" is καταργέω (*katargeo*) meaning to render inactive, idle, useless, or ineffective.[207] Hence, one could say that the Law was stripped of its power over a believer as a rule of life, or better yet, it was put out of business in this regard. This word is found in the aorist, passive, indicative, indicating that this rendering inactive or idle of one's relationship to the Law happened at a point in time in reality and was enacted upon by an outside source (namely God). Paul clearly states that the Law is no longer useful in the believer's life. The Law is said to have "held" (κατέχω – *katecho*, meaning to hold fast, retain,

[207] Zodhiates, The Complete Word Study Dictionary: New Testament, 841.

hold down, quash, or suppress)[208] believers. This word is used in Romans 1:18 to describe how ungodly men "suppress" (**katecho**) the truth. This word is used by Paul in the imperfect, passive, indicative, indicating that the Law used to suppress believers in the past continually; this was the reality of the believers' situation before being saved. Although the believers' position in relationship to the Law has changed, they can still go back to the Law as their rule of life. Paul's main thrust in this passage is that if believers do this, it is extremely unprofitable for them and dangerous to their growth in maturity. God's whole purpose in changing believers' relationship to the Law was not merely because individuals could not keep the Law, but, because it was when individuals try to keep it, they are unfruitful to Him and are held back by the Law. God has a different method for fulfilling the Law's righteousness in believers' lives, and it is not through believers keeping the Law.

In an attempt to introduce "why" the believer should still strive to keep the Law, Piper introduces the "New Covenant." Piper quotes Jeremiah 31:31-34 and then states the following two points: "1. We learn that in the new covenant the Law will no longer mainly be external, written on stone (that's what "letter" means), but will be mainly internal, written on the heart (verse 33). In other words, the decisive thing about the Law will no longer be that it is a *demand* from outside, but it will be a *desire* from inside. 2. Or, as verse 34 puts it, knowing God will not be an external command so much as an internal experience."[209] Moreover, he says the following elsewhere in the same article: "And, therefore, finally the Law of God is being written on your heart. The will of God does not crush you from outside with its demand for unattainable perfection. That Law is satisfied in Jesus. Now the will of God rises in your heart as the Spirit transforms your desires and makes you free."[210] This would make very good sense if the New Covenant were for the church-age; however as one will see with straight-forward hermeneutics and simple observation, this is not the case.[211]

First of all, if one simply observes "who" the beneficiaries of the New Covenant are, one will notice that they are identified as the "house of Israel"

---

[208] Zodiahtes, The Complete Word Study Dictionary: New Testament, 850.

[209] Piper, "Dead to the Law, Serving in the Spirit, Part 1."

[210] Piper, "Dead to the Law, Serving in the Spirit, Part 1."

[211] See Dr. Christopher Cone's book entitled An Introduction to the New Covenant (Tyndale Seminary Press) for a good handling of all of the views by evangelical scholars on the New Covenant.

and "the house of Judah" in the Jeremiah passage. This does not include Gentile believers. Some of the same benefits that the Jews will receive in their New Covenant are similar to the benefits Gentile believers receive in the dispensation of grace — namely forgiveness of sins and the indwelling Holy Spirit (see Ezekiel 11:19, 36:26-27). However, the New Covenant and the dispensation of grace are not the same. If one interprets these covenants with a literal hermeneutic, one is forced to recognize that the New Covenant applies only to the physical descendants of Abraham. Ezekiel 36:27 states, "I will put My Spirit within you and cause you to walk in My statutes, and you will keep My judgments and do *them.*" Furthermore, Ezekiel writes, "Then you shall dwell in the **land** that I gave to your fathers." This is clearly referring to the nation of Israel — the final fulfillment of the Palestinian Land Covenant. Additionally, because of the language used in the New Covenant passages, it is clear that the saved Jewish human beings will have a favorable disposition towards the Lord during the Millennial Kingdom. This will be unique and distinct from any other time in human history, including the Church-age.[212] Piper, however, uses this very combination of passages to teach that the believer can now keep the Law because he or she has the right inward desires based on the results of the New Covenant. If Piper continued to read down through the rest of Romans 7, he would notice that the apostle Paul had the "right inward desires," but those inward desires to keep God's Law were not effective in enabling him to keep the righteousness found in the Law. This is why Paul emphasizes that a believer needs a new relationship to the Law — one of death to the law.

To his credit, Piper attempts to make a scriptural conclusion as to why the believer should be under Law. MacArthur, however, makes no such

---

[212] Jeremiah 31:34 says, "No more shall every man teach his neighbor...saying know the Lord, for they shall all know Me." – This is unique because in the church-age, gifted evangelists and pastor-teachers have been given to the body to teach the body (Ephesians 4:11-16), implying that church-age believers **NEED** teaching! Jeremiah 31:33 says, "I will put my Law in their minds and write it on their hearts." This is most likely the "reason" they will not need to be taught in the day of the implementation of the New Covenant. Ezekiel 36:27 says, "I will put My Spirit within you and **CAUSE YOU** to walk in My statutes, and you **WILL KEEP** My judgements and **DO THEM**," – Notice, God will be the one causing the saved Jewish person's obedience and it is here (in the Millennial Kingdom, with the New Covenant enacted) that their obedience is guaranteed. This is why it is so IMPORTANT to have an accurate hermeneutic for this passage especially. This is NOT referring to church-age saints!

attempt to tie Romans 7 together with the new covenant. He states, "We still serve the law. In fact, we serve it better than we could before we were redeemed. Because we serve not the letter of the law but the spirit."[213] Moreover, as previously quoted, MacArthur states, "So somebody asks the question: if we're free from the law as Christians, is the law binding on us? The answer is no and yes. It is not binding in the sense that our acceptance with God depends on it, it is binding in the sense that our new life seeks to serve it. You see, the law couldn't save you because you couldn't keep it. Now that God saved you, the law can't condemn you and for the first time in your life by the power of the Holy Spirit you can keep it. So we're not under the law condemnation but we serve God's law out of the depths of a committed heart."[214] If this does not miss Paul's point in Romans 7:1-6, what possibly could? Paul specifically describes believers' new relationship to the Law as being one that is no longer binding. Paul does not want believers returning to their husband (the Law), leaving their marriage to the risen Christ. In fact, this by definition would be adultery.

How then does God make believers righteous? If they are dead to the Law, does that mean they are antinomian lawbreakers, as lordship teachers would suggest that free grace proponents teach? Lordship and commitment salvation advocates fear this licentiousness, and hence they promote a gospel of surrender, commitment, and Law-keeping to become holy. However, they are missing a very simple point: the very Holy Spirit who wrote the Law and the very Son of God who kept the Law perfectly are both permanently indwelling each believer. So, should the believer look at the Law for his guidance and daily life, or should he depend upon the Holy Spirit to produce the life of Christ in him or her? The answer is simple. Ron Merryman summarizes it this way:

"That we are 'not under the Law' **does not** mean that the moral absolutes of the Law are negated or done away. The moral absolutes of the Law have **always** been applicable. It has **always** been sin to lie, steal, commit adultery, covet, etc. Such acts and mental attitudes were wrong before the Law was given; they are still wrong. 'Not under the Law' does not mean that these defining absolutes no longer exist. But the believer actually has the Holy Spirit living within. His/her responsibility is to the very Spirit of Christ who wrote

---

[213] MacArthur, "Dead to the Law."
[214] MacArthur, "Dead to the Law."

the Law, rather than a list of do's and don'ts. Grace provides the administrative controls in the believer's life."[215]

This battle between going back to the Law and walking in the Spirit is clearly delineated at the end of Romans 7 and in the beginning of Romans 8. Paul, in absolute frustration, cries out in Romans 7:24: "O wretched man that I am! Who will deliver me from this body of death?" The word translated "wretched" comes from a root word meaning "suffering," and it means afflicted, wretched, miserable, or distressed.[216] In fact, the same word is used of the lukewarm Laodicean church in Revelation 3:17. Vincent's Word Studies says this word originally meant "wretched through the exhaustion of hard labor." Paul was laboring for sanctification via law-keeping, and he could not figure out why he could not execute the desires of his new nature when he did indeed love God's law. In utmost despair, Paul finally realizes that it was not a "what" (a Law) that would deliver him from sin's power, but rather it was a "who" (the Lord Jesus Christ). Thus, Paul says, " **WHO** will deliver me from this body of death?" Deliverance is found in a person, not in a method, or in one's best efforts to keep the Law.

In Romans 8:4, the person of the Holy Spirit comes into play. The very Spirit of the Lord Jesus Christ indwells believers to accomplish something for believers that they cannot accomplish themselves by looking at the Law, and He desires to produce the righteous requirements of the Law in and through believers. Notice something very unique about Romans 8:4 – the text does not tell us that the Spirit of God enables believers to keep the Law as lordship proponents teach. It is a subtle and yet very important distinction – the Holy Spirit desires to fulfill the righteous **requirement** of the law in us. Romans 8:4 says, "That the righteous requirement of the law might be fulfilled in us who do not walk according to the flesh but according to the Spirit." In Georgia, most highways have a speed limit of 70 MPH. If one were to drive a car whose speed was limited to 70 MPH by certain internal controls installed by the manufacturer, as long as he or she was in that car, he or she would never break the law on the highway. Now, each time one drives that specific car, he or she will abide by the speed limit, as the car has internal, built-in controls to obey the Law. It is not because one is looking at the speed limit all the time, looking at his or her dashboard, or making sure he or she does

[215] Merryman, The Believer and the Mosaic Law: Growth Truth for Believers, 16.
[216] Zodhiates, The Complete Word Study Dictionary: New Testament, 5005.

not have a lead foot. Notice the spiritual connection – when believers walk by means of the Spirit, they will fulfill the righteous requirements of the law in them, not because **THEY** are trying to keep the Law, but because they are relying upon the Spirit of God and are controlled and/or influenced by Him as they live life.

In Galatians 5:9, Paul states, "A little leaven leavens the whole lump." This is what a legalistic sanctification and a "works gospel" do. Because of their lordship commitment/surrender gospel, lordship teachers create undefinable standards for the Christian to meet, such as the Law of God, which by definition is impossible to keep. Clearly, according to Romans 7, God is doing something completely different than law-keeping for the Christian to grow in holiness. Spirituality is accomplished as a believer walks in dependence upon the indwelling Holy Spirit of God. This same Holy Spirit is the very One who wrote the Law, who knows the mind of God, and can produce the life of Christ in the believer. This very life is the living Word of God!

CHAPTER 5
Christ-Centric or Man-Centric?

In Numbers 21:4-9, during the time of the Israelites' wandering in the wilderness, an event in history is recorded. This event happens towards the end of the Israelites' time of wandering (the end of the forty years). Numbers 21:4-5 reads: "Then they journeyed from Mount Hor by the Way of the Red Sea, to go around the land of Edom; and the soul of the people became very discouraged on the way. And the people spoke against God and against Moses: 'Why have you brought us up out of Egypt to die in the wilderness? For *there is* no food and no water, and our soul loathes this worthless bread.'" Regarding this area of the desert, Keil and Delitzsch comment the following: "It is, '. . . a horrible desert, with a loose sandy soil, and drifts of granite and other stones, where terrible sandstorms sometimes arise from the neighborhood of the Red Sea . . .'"[217] In the Israelites' minds, they had a lot to complain about, so they did not hold back on their grumblings. In fact, they complained against God and against Moses because they had no food (except for manna, which they despised) and no water. As a result of their complaining, God did the following, as seen in Numbers 21:6: "So the Lord sent fiery serpents among the people, and they bit the people; and many of the people of Israel died." It appears that as soon as the people realized the seriousness of the snakes and how they could harm them, they knew "who" to turn their gaze upon. In fact, it was the very ones whom they had complained about only moments before: Moses and God.

Numbers 21:7 reads, "Therefore the people came to Moses, and said, 'We have sinned, for we have spoken against the Lord and against you; pray to the Lord that He take away the serpents from us.' So, Moses prayed for the people." It is wise to notice a couple of things from the text. First, God does not answer the people's request to "take away the serpents from us." God devises a way to be rescued or healed from the serpents' bites, but He does not remove the source of judgment as the method of deliverance. Second, notice that Moses' prayer was not enough to deliver the people from the presence of the serpents, nor was it enough to heal the people from their

---

[217] C.F. Keil, F. Delitzch, <u>Vol. 1: Commentary on the Old Testament: Pentateuch</u>, (Peabody, MA: Hendrickson Publishers, 1996), 745.

snake bites. God was very clear in His instructions to the Israelites about how they could be delivered or healed from the serpents' bites. Numbers 21:8-9 clearly records the outcome for those who approached God in His way: "Then the Lord said to Moses, 'Make a fiery *serpent,* and set it on a pole; and it shall be that everyone who is bitten, when he looks at it, shall live.' So, Moses made a bronze serpent, and put it on a pole; and so, it was, if a serpent had bitten anyone, when he looked at the bronze serpent, he lived."

The story is very clear, and God's instructions are equally as clear. Once Moses made the bronze serpent on the pole, there was only one method of salvation from the serpents' bites — to "look" at the bronze serpent. If a bitten Israelite refused to look at Moses' bronze serpent because he thought Moses' idea was ridiculous, unable to save, not hard enough, or just plain weird, it is clear the Israelite would have died that day. In fact, none of the Israelites' own human-reliant strategies could have saved them, and no amount of past contrition or future promises could deliver them either. The verdict was in — they deserved to die, but God provided the means, the solution, by which they could escape death.

What relevance does this story have today, specifically in relationship to lordship salvation? In John 3:14-16, Jesus Himself makes the connection when He says, "And as Moses lifted up the serpent in the wilderness, even so must the Son of Man be lifted up, that whoever believes in Him should not perish but have eternal life. For God so loved the world that He gave His only begotten Son, that whoever believes in Him should not perish but have everlasting life." In this statement, Jesus uses a simile comparing Moses' raising up of the serpent in the wilderness and His own death on the cross. Just as the Israelites were to simply "look at" Moses' bronze serpent as their only means of deliverance and healing, so one today must simply "believe/trust in/rely upon" Jesus' death on the cross as the only means of salvation from sin's penalty (death). The New Testament states, in over 160 verses, that the only pre-requisite for salvation is faith alone, which is in complete agreement with the simile that Jesus uses regarding Moses and bronze serpent.[218]

These parallels are essential to note and hold profound truth. An Israelite could do nothing to save him or herself from the poisonous snake bite, just as a sinner can do nothing to save him or herself from the penalty of

---

[218] J.B. Hixson, "150+ Verses Proving Justification by Faith Alone."

sin. Notice the Israelite was not commanded to submit or surrender to receive the full benefit of looking at the bronze serpent, just as the sinner is not commanded to submit, commit, or surrender to the lordship mastery of Christ in order for his or her belief to benefit him eternally. The Israelite's whole focus was to be on God's provision (the bronze serpent) rather than his or her own promises to do better. In the same way, the sinner's whole focus is to be on God's provision (Jesus Christ's death on the cross and His resurrection) rather than on his or her own promises of obedience and submission. In both circumstances, the focus is on God's work, God's provision, and God's method of dealing with the problem of sin and death. Mankind's only part involves a looking away from oneself and not a looking to or at oneself. Both the Israelite and the sinner are to look to God's solution and His solution alone!

Contrary to Jesus' words in John 3, lordship teachers instruct Christians to focus on their own works as well as on Christ's work. It is no wonder that lordship teachers struggle with their own works and God's work in their own Christian lives. This impacts everything they believe in regard to the Christian life. For instance, MacArthur says, "Where you land on the lordship question will also have far-reaching implications for your views on assurance, faith, repentance, eternal rewards, human depravity, the role of the moral law, and a host of other crucial doctrines."[219] Galatians 5:9, which says, "A little leaven leavens the whole lump," is definitely true, as the lordship view spreads into many other areas of Christian life teaching. MacArthur wrongly concludes that it is the no-lordship doctrine that taints all other areas of soteriology, rather than recognizing there is an error with his own view of the Christian life.

Consider the following real-life testimonies from people who have been negatively impacted by the false teaching of lordship salvation. These individuals were not initially taught that all one needs to do is to look to and rely on Jesus to be saved, and there is nothing that can make one lose that salvation. The following is one account a gentleman shared with the author about his and his wife's experiences with lordship salvation. He details below:

---

[219] John MacArthur, "A 15-Year Retrospective on the Lordship Controversy," Grace to You, accessed July 1, 2020, http://www.gty.org/resources/articles/A100/a-15year-retrospective-on-the-lordship-controversy.

My wife started to believe that she could lose her salvation in her teenage years. She did not think that God would take it from her, but she thought that she could reject God to the point that she would cause herself to lose her salvation. She had a very close friend that introduced her to the free grace gospel and eternal security. When her friend shared this with her, she convinced my wife that she was once saved, always saved. This truth not only changed her life, it completely freed her from the bondage she had been under. Two verses were very instrumental in showing her the truth. They are John 10:28 and 1 Corinthians 3:15.

When I was in the bus ministry many years ago, I would use door-to-door visitation to share the gospel with the children's parents who we picked up every Sunday. On one of these visits, as I was sharing the gospel of grace with one of the parents, the lady started crying because she could not believe that when she trusted in Christ as her Savior, she was then eternally saved forever and could never lose it. She was so released and kept saying, "This is incredible! I feel a sense of freedom."

On another occasion, I was sharing the teaching of eternal security with a co-worker and helping him understand that the Christian walk was the same as the believer's salvation. I shared that it is not based on merit, but it is based on accepting what God says to be true. As I did this for several months, another person that worked with us listened to what I was sharing with this brother. This brother that I shared God's free gift with finally saw clearly the truth in the Scriptures and left the denomination he was in and started attending a free grace church. He began to grow in grace and realized his walk with the Lord was no longer dependent on his works, but by his walk of faith with his Lord. What is interesting about this story is that the other person who was listening to our conversation crossed paths with me 10 years later and wanted to have lunch with me. During lunch, he shared with me that he had gone back and looked at the Scriptures I had shared, and he became totally convinced that he was once saved and always saved, and he stopped living in fear of losing his salvation. He wanted to have lunch with me to thank me for sharing the truth of God's Word. What is amazing about any of this is that we never know how God will use what we share to help free others from the bondage of legalism.

The following is another story from the author's friend, who is currently a pastor. He describes his own negative experience and exposure to lordship salvation below:

Defeated. The best days of my Christian life, growing up under Lordship Salvation, were in defeat. Of course, life was always in motion — moving between periods of self-righteousness for a few weeks, followed by colossal spiritual failure, and then into defeat and spiritual despair. I was confident that I had lost my salvation (or never had it) about twice a month (or any time a pretty girl walked by — whichever came first). I would skip along through the times when I thought I was doing awfully well and even believed that God must be impressed with me, but then the times of failure invoked me to sorrow and deep spiritual depression. I would lay in my bed for hours, weeping and bemoaning my own inability to live the life of perfection that I believed God expected of anyone whom He would save. Then, as weeping only endures for a night, I would say to myself: 'Well, maybe it wasn't all that bad.' I could be humble for a day, prideful for a week, and then back in tears by the end of the month. This cycle continued unabated throughout my college experience until a dear friend shared Watchman Nee's Sit, Walk, Stand with me and after I read The Normal Christian Life. These books were the first chance I had ever had to be exposed to the truth of the believer's position in Christ and to salvation in all three phases by grace alone, through faith alone, and in Christ alone. It took me years to work through the lasting impacts spiritual abuse had had on my life at the hands of lordship teachers like MacArthur and Sproul. However, not long after this, the Lord brought me to a good, solid, Bible-teaching church, and finally I understood why the message about our new life in Christ really is good news.

Below is yet another account from a woman who was encouraged by the free grace message after having been exposed to lordship teaching:

I remember the pastor saying the following many times from the pulpit: "Jesus can't be your Savior if he's not your Lord." It would leave me thinking, "What does that mean? I think He's my Lord. What if He's not totally my Lord?" It took the teaching of a clear gospel for me to realize that my former way of thinking had meant that Jesus' work on the cross was not enough, and that I must add to it by "making Him my Lord." I'm so very grateful to have now learned that it is simply my faith in the finished work of Jesus that saves me and nothing more.

Another gentleman, a dear friend of the author and former pastor, recounts the following negative experience with lordship salvation teachers and concepts:

In my early Christian life, I was exposed to the teachings of Ray Comfort in his "Way of the Master" series on evangelism. I remember him saying something to the effect that "if you are not doing evangelism, you are probably not saved." As a new and earnest believer, I took that concept to heart. I began to do evangelism out of a motive to prove to myself and to God that I was saved. My motivation was not out of love or concern for the lost, but instead it was for myself. It was so I could feel better about my relationship with God. After growing in my understanding and discernment of what constitutes salvation (justification) and what constitutes living the Christian life (sanctification), I realized that Ray Comfort was blending these two things together and thereby doing damage to both justification and sanctification. Also, I received additional discipleship in the area of justification, which brought me great joy and security in knowing that I was saved by Christ the moment I believed in Him. I learned that evangelism had no bearing or indication on my salvation, and I was safe and secure because my faith was in Christ and His work on the cross. After being cleared up on the issues surrounding Ray Comfort's teaching that had previously given me a false motivation for evangelism, I began to desire to do evangelism because I wanted to share the love and grace I had discovered through Christ. It was a night and day difference.

Moreover, Dr. Frank B. Minirth, who is a Diplomat of the American Board of Psychiatry and Neurology, the President of Minirth-Meier Clinics, an Associate Professor of Pastoral Ministries at Dallas Theological Seminary, author or co-author of 37 books, and a co-host on radio and television had this to say about the negative impact lordship salvation had on one of his patients:

One of my psychiatric patients had been exposed to the grace-plus system, and combined with her own obsessive-compulsive personality, she succumbed to disabling guilt, frustration, and disillusionment. She stated, "I'm going to hell. I just know it. I haven't done enough right." I asked her to picture Christ on the Cross, to picture each of her sins driving a spike into His hand, and finally to visualize carrying all of her guilt up to the Cross and giving it to Christ. She had an anguished demeanor. I shared John 6:37 and Ephesians 2:8-9, and explained that what we do and don't do in the Christian life is not based on a "brownie-point" system, but on faith in Christ as our

Savior. Soon a serene, peaceful look came over her face. I had introduced her to grace.[220]

Furthermore, Dr. Minirth goes on to write the following:
Untold psychological damage is done when an individual feels he is accepted on a conditional basis. This may be expressed in a contradictory message, such as "I love you, but you must..." It produces a paradox that makes choice impossible. It is a "double-bind" message to combine grace with merit. This message asks a person to do two conflicting things. By definition, grace is God's unmerited favor, a free gift (eternal life—Romans 6:23). This means that one cannot earn grace because this, would contradict the definition. Thus, when a minister or priest asks someone to do something for the grace of God, he has just presented the individual with an impossible choice. If the individual chooses grace, he cannot do anything for it. Yet, the minister has told him that he must do something. The person cannot win!...Of all personality types the *obsessive-compulsives* are the most susceptible to lordship theology. Lordship doctrine drives them to seek perfection (which is impossible in this life), driving them down the road to bondage. These individuals are over conscientious, over dutiful, and perfectionistic, always striving for 99%. Lordship teaching drives them to strive for 99.9%, making them even *more* obsessive and scrupulous regarding their values (far beyond the demands of faith and culture). Because they expect too much out of themselves, they frequently become angry with themselves, which results in depression.[221]

Moreover, Shawn Lazar, the Director of Publications for Grace Evangelical Society (GES) recounts a story from a sermon he listened to regarding the negative impact of lordship salvation. He shares the following:
I heard a lordship pastor tell the story of talking to two sisters who recognized him at a local Christian bookstore. The sisters asked for advice about their mother who was dying in hospice. They said that caring for their mother was becoming more troubling, not only because she was dying, but because she would say disturbing things. The preacher didn't give any specific examples of what the dying mother said, but the

---

[220] Frank B. Minirth, "The Psychological Effects of Lordship Salvation," *GES (Grace Evangelical Society)*, last modified September 1, 1993, accessed October 21, 2020, https://faithalone.org/journal-articles/the-psychological-effects-of-lordship-salvation/.
[221] Minirth, "The Psychological Effects of Lordship Salvation."

impression was she was saying *unchristian* things, and that made it harder on the sisters. The sisters asked what to think of that? The preacher's answer was generic—that God is with us during times of calamity, working all things for our good (another misapplication), etc.

But then he went off on a tangent. He started talking about "genuine" faith and "genuine" believers going through calamity… "Genuine faith always gets back up," he said. "Genuine believers might fall down and fall again, but they don't stay down. They get back up—always." …It sounded like the mother's body was shutting down. She was probably delusional and slowly losing her mind. The last words she uttered might have been sinful, even blasphemous, but was she culpable? Not if she was not in her right mind. But even if she were culpable, would her words prove she was not a genuine believer? Would they prove she was never saved to begin with? Are we saved by faith *plus* keeping our tongue under control until we die?[222]

Brandon Burdette, a writer who lives in Los Angeles, California, is yet another person impacted by lordship theology. He shares the following:

It happened on a late Sunday afternoon, between services. The elders brought a teenage girl named Esther before the membership to have her sin exposed. Esther was a nice, quiet girl who regularly came to church with her polite, Spanish-speaking family. She was active in the children's ministry and in the choir. Up to this point, nobody in the church had any reason to doubt she was a saved person. But she had recently become pregnant by a boy from her high school and felt very embarrassed about it. An elder escorted Esther up to the pulpit, where the pastor waited. She was sniffling. The church was silent. She sheepishly looked at the floor. The pastor began to describe her circumstances and told us she wished to repent of her sin publicly, *unto salvation*. He went on to explain that Esther's sin indicated she had not been regenerated. He announced, "Esther wishes to profess her newfound faith in Jesus Christ before you all." She did this while weeping. She said she had truly put her trust in Christ this time. From now on she'd live a life of obedience. Members solemnly clapped and murmured Amens. As for me, I couldn't believe my eyes and ears! I sat

[222] Shawn Lazar, "Lordship Salvation is a Poor Comfort for a Dying Relative," *GES (Grace Evangelical Society)*, last modified November 14, 2019, accessed October 21, 2020, https://faithalone.org/blog/lordship-salvation-is-poor-comfort-for-a-dying-relative/.

dumbfounded in my pew. Questions started racing through my mind. "What about King David and his impregnating Bathsheba? Hadn't he been regenerate when he impregnated her? Indeed, hadn't he already written some of the Psalms? And what about Samson? Doesn't the book of Judges say he was a Nazarite unto God from the womb, and that he womanized among harlots? Hebrews 11 says Samson was a great hero of the faith. And how about Solomon?" …I took my questions and thoughts to the pastor later that evening, to no avail. I can only pray that Esther believed the saving message at some point and is free from Lordship Salvation today.[223]

Similarly, Roscoe Barnes III relayed his own personal experience of leaving lordship salvation theology in *Grace In Focus* magazine. He writes:

Then one day, the light came on. My friend, Ron Bupp, had been talking to an inmate who asked about eternal security. Bupp had directed him to the doctrine of justification by faith which excluded works. "So, Chaplain," the inmate asked him, "Since salvation is not based on works, if I could lose it, then it would be based on works, wouldn't it?" That question pierced my heart. I was so moved by it, I rushed home and went back to Romans. I stopped at Romans 3:21-22: But now apart from the Law the righteousness of God has been manifested, being witnessed by the Law and the Prophets, even the righteousness of God through faith in Jesus Christ for all those who believe; for there is no distinction. As I read that passage, along with Romans 4, I started to see the truth of the grace gospel. For the first time in my life, I began to see that salvation is by faith alone in Christ alone. I thought. 'Why didn't I see this 20 years ago?' For the next few months, I lived in Romans 3 and 4. Because Jesus promises eternal life to all who simply believe in Him, I came to realize that to doubt eternal security was to question justification by faith alone. Furthermore, to reject the doctrine of eternal security would be to reject the free grace of God.[224]

Another man, a dear friend of the author, also was negatively impacted by lordship salvation. In a personal email to the author, he recounted the following:

---

[223] Brandon Burdette, "The Harsh Hand of Lordship Theology," *GES (Grace Evangelical Society)*, last modified November 1, 2017, accessed October 21, 2020, https://faithalone.org/grace-in-focus-articles/the-harsh-hand-of-lordship-theology/.

[224] Roscoe Barnes III, "A Pentecostal Finds Grace," *GES (Grace Evangelical Society)*, last modified 2010, accessed October 21, 2020, https://faithalone.org/magazine/y2003/03C2.html.

I was brought up in an evangelical Christian church. When I was a very young boy, my Sunday School teachers taught me that I needed to ask Jesus to come into my heart and forgive my sins. So, although it seemed strange to ask someone big like Jesus to come into my little heart, I did this whenever my teacher said that we should (which was just about every Sunday over a two-to-three-year period). Thinking about it now, I realize that I must have literally asked Jesus into my heart hundreds of times! No matter how often I did, however, I was never certain that He had really come in or that I was truly forgiven.

I later learned that the concept of asking Jesus into your heart is entirely absent in the Scriptures and is, in fact, a poor substitute (much more difficult for a child to understand) for what it means to "believe on the Lord Jesus Christ." Revelation 3:20, which is often quoted to support the idea of asking Jesus into your heart, says nothing about how a person receives salvation, forgiveness of sins, or eternal life. Even a casual reading of this verse in its context reveals that it was written to the believers in the Church of Laodicea and speaks of Christ's desire to come into the assembly and fellowship with those who are already His own.

When I was seven years old, I told my dad that I wasn't really sure that I was saved. He responded by telling me to pray the "sinner's prayer" (or some variation of it) and to ask God for forgiveness. So, at his prompting, I prayed, repeating word for word what he told me to say. He then congratulated me and assured me that I was now truly saved. However, over time, I could see no significant change in my life, and I had no real assurance. I continued to disobey my parents (not always, but often enough) I would constantly get into fights with my younger brother, and I would sometimes use the bad words that I learned from the other kids in the neighborhood. I also found church to be boring and had little interest in praying or reading my Bible.

The so-called "sinner's prayer," in its various forms, is found nowhere in the Scriptures nor is it an adequate or accurate representation of what it means to "believe on the Lord Jesus Christ." It is my opinion that many people (including myself) have prayed "the" prayer without any real understanding of the gospel of grace and Christ's substitutionary sacrifice on the cross on their behalf.

By the time I became a teenager, I was in constant doubt about my salvation and was confused about what I actually needed to do to become a 'true' Christian. I was being told a variety of different things from Sunday school teachers and youth leaders, some of which were actually contradictory. For example, I was told that in order to be saved I needed to follow Christ, be more committed to Him, and meet the qualifications of being a disciple (i.e., deny myself, take up my cross, and bear fruit, etc.) but that salvation was a "free gift." I was also told that I needed to make a public commitment by going forward to the front of the church when the pastor made the appeal for us to commit our lives to Christ (the so-called "altar call").

It is very common for pastors and teachers to distort the simple and straightforward message of the gospel by adding various conditions and requirements that apply only to the process of spiritual growth and a life of discipleship. The cost of living as a disciple or follower of Christ over time can be very high. Many have lost their lives and many more have suffered great persecution. In stark contrast, salvation is "the gift of God," freely given, without cost, to the worst of sinners who will simply believe the gospel message that Christ died and rose again on their behalf. This salvation was purchased once and for all by the precious blood of Christ, which was shed for us long before we were ever born. "For by grace are you saved through faith...not by works." Personal devotion, acts of contrition, and so-called "public professions" have no place or part in our justification before God.

Having been told that I needed to "take a stand" for Christ publicly, I consulted with my dad about this. He said that the best way to make a public commitment was to be baptized. So, at the next opportunity, I was baptized and gave a spoken testimony to the fact that I had prayed to receive Christ when I was seven years old. At my baptism, my dad also testified that he remembered the day that I prayed and was "saved."

When Paul wrote to the Corinthians that "Christ called me, not to baptize, but to preach the gospel," he made a clear and obvious distinction between the external rite of water baptism and the straightforward message of the gospel, which is: "Christ died for our sins...and rose again the third day." Faith alone in Jesus Christ and what He has already accomplished for us by His death and resurrection is the sole condition set forth in the Bible for receiving forgiveness of sins and eternal salvation. Simple, childlike faith in Christ is presented well over 150 times in the New Testament as the only way a person can be made right with God.

Over the next several years, I was actively involved in our church and church youth group. I regularly attended Christian summer camps, retreats, conferences, seminars and evangelistic crusades. I also listened to Christian radio on a daily basis. As a result of these experiences, I was exposed to many different teachers, preachers, evangelists and youth leaders and was hearing a variety of explanations as to what was required for a person to receive forgiveness of sins and eternal life. For example, I was told that I needed to "give up evil habits," "turn from my sin," and "live a life of submission and obedience to Christ." These things were presented, not just as things a *Christian* should do, but as conditions that must be met in order for a person to receive salvation.

On the occasions when faith in Jesus Christ were mentioned, the word "faith" was often redefined as referring to a *life-change* or a decision to follow Christ in constant obedience, etc. In direct contradiction to the overall teaching of Scripture (and in contradiction to the author's intended meaning), some have attempted to use the book of James to re-define faith as "works." A careful study of James, however, reveals that James is written exclusively to brothers (i.e., believers) and not to so-called "professors." In other words, James is not telling people how to get saved (his readers were already saved), but rather he is telling them how to live by faith as believers. James was emphasizing that these Christians should have a *walk* of faith and not just a *talk* of faith. He wanted these believers to understand that a life of faith should be characterized by actions that glorify God. Being very practical, James made it clear that these Christians should be meeting the physical needs of their fellow believers and not just talking about it!

While I was in high school, I attended a weekend church retreat. The guest speaker was a powerful, gifted, dynamic communicator who would speak twice a day, holding us as it were *spellbound* for 90 minutes at a time. This was no small feat considering that most of us were teenagers and there to have a good time. This man preached against sin and complacency and said that many of us, perhaps most of us, were simply *playing the part* of being a Christian. He made it clear that unless we were totally "sold out" to the lordship of Christ and totally submissive to Him as the Master of our lives, we were not truly saved. As I listened carefully to the man as he was speaking, I realized that my commitment to Christ was not always what it should be and that my walk with Him was inconsistent at best. I also knew that I often struggled with impure thoughts, and my attitude toward my parents and school teachers was less than exemplary.

After one of the meetings, I approached the speaker and confessed to him that I wasn't sure that I was saved because of what he had been teaching us about the necessity of having a greater commitment and a deeper devotion to Christ. He told me that I had certainly not been saved at a younger age because I had never totally submitted my life to Jesus and had never truly died to self. He told me that what I really needed was self-denial, self-crucifixion, and a life of sacrificial obedience.

During this period of my life, I was also being strongly influenced by a dynamic, authoritative radio Bible teacher. This man, a well-known pastor, affirmed and reaffirmed what the speaker at the retreat had said. For example, he said things like becoming converted is not simply a matter of believing that Christ died for your sins, and that true biblical faith includes so much more than trusting in Christ alone. He taught that faith involves the entire surrender of one's will to the will of Christ and a total turning away from sin. He also said that a life of obedience must necessarily follow any decision to follow Christ, and no one can truly call himself a Christian who is not entirely yielded to the lordship of Christ.

After listening to this teacher regularly on the radio and reading some of what he had written and, after considering what I had heard at the church retreat, I became convinced that it would be impossible for me, or anyone else, to know with certainty that they have eternal life. If what these men were teaching were true, no one could truly know that they were saved. After much thought, I came to the conclusion that anyone (including these teachers) who were honest with themselves would have to admit that their submission and devotion to Christ was inconsistent at best. I also wondered if these teachers who demanded my *all* were actually totally submitted to God themselves.

The Bible tells us, "The heart is deceitful above all else and desperately wicked, who can know it?" In other words, because of our blind spots and our inherent inability to recognize our own faults, we often deceive ourselves into thinking we are better or more obedient to Christ than we actually are. King David prayed, "Lord, save me from my secret sins" and from "presumptuous sins." The Bible makes it clear that we are often self-deceived and unaware of our own motives. It has been stated (correctly I think) that in general we are unaware of the majority of our true motives and blind to the sinful tendencies of our hearts. The Bible makes it clear that there is no one righteous in God's sight, and that the very best we have to offer is offensive to God. Our deepest devotion and our sincerest efforts add up to less than nothing when it comes to how we are saved. Justification is by faith alone in Christ alone, totally apart from our personal dedication and devotion. Our greatest efforts and our highest spiritual attainments are nothing but "filthy rags" in God's sight.

I will end now by telling you that God actually used all the false teaching that I was exposed to as a young man to *drive me* to the truth of God's Word. In my early 20's, I became so disturbed by what I was hearing from these teachers and many others who were adding to and/or distorting the gospel message that I became passionate about studying the Scriptures. I spent approximately three years constantly reading and memorizing the primary gospel passages. In the process, I learned the truth that is so clearly spelled out in Romans 3:21-4:9 and numerous other passages that Christ had atoned for my sins on the cross once and for all, and He had become my substitutionary sacrifice by paying the full and final price for my salvation. I knew that I was a sinner and studying the opening verses of Romans chapter 3 confirmed this beyond all doubt. I also understood, clearly and objectively for the first time, that forgiveness of sins and the imputed righteousness that God offers as a free gift is received only by faith. By God's infinite grace, I clearly comprehended the meaning of the words — "This righteousness of God comes through faith in Jesus Christ to all who believe," and I believed in Jesus Christ alone, casting aside all of my so-called devotion, dedication, and submission. Now I know that my salvation has been procured and secured forever by the blood of Christ! This is my testimony, and this is what I now celebrate every day, as I bask in God's grace and the perfect righteousness that has been imputed to me by grace through faith alone.

So, as one can see from the aforementioned testimonies, lordship teaching can have a long-lasting, negative impact on believers. It is truly tragic to read and hear of sincere believers, who desire to pursue the Lord, feeling beat down, unworthy, and unsure of their salvation. Praise God that the Savior "saves" those who believe in Him and that the Savior also "keeps them saved." The true tragedy of those who are negatively impacted by lordship teaching is that they forget the high value of the finished work of Jesus Christ. They forget everything He accomplished for them 2,000 years ago when He died for their sins and rose again.

CHAPTER 6
Conclusion And Wrap-Up

The purpose of this book was to evaluate, critique, and offer a biblical response to the negative impact of the lordship gospel on the Christian's life. Again, lordship salvation is simply defined as the following: the salvation response to the gospel, which in addition to simple faith in the person and work of Christ on the cross, teaches that one must submit or yield to Christ's lordship in terms of mastery. In other words, lordship salvation states that both faith and surrender/commitment are pre-requisites for being saved from the penalty of sin. Much as a home built on an unstable foundation or on shifting soil will eventually show its poor foundation through visible cracks in the house's walls, the lordship gospel will reveal its faulty foundation through cracks in one's Christian life. The three major cracks or areas of concern include the following: (1) lack of eternal security and assurance of salvation for the believer, (2) sanctification focused on the believer, rather than God, and (3) legalism in the Christian life

The First Superstructure Crack: Eternal Security

The first exposed crack with the lordship foundation is the believer's eternal security. While both lordship proponents and true grace advocates consider eternal security a biblical doctrine, there is disagreement as to what constitutes someone's eternal security. There is not one lordship teacher who could ever teach with sincerity of heart that someone is truly saved before he or she dies. In fact, in order to maintain doctrinal consistency, lordship teachers have to teach that one "might have" eternal life because their teaching on perseverance results in not truly knowing for sure. Because they require commitment and making Jesus Lord to be saved, people are never able to reach full assurance of their eternal destiny. The lordship doctrine takes the focus off the work of Christ and His payment for the penalty of sin (death), and it puts the focus back on sinners and their ability to continue in their commitment to God. The irony of all this is that lordship teachers tout their gospel as "God-centered" or "God-centric" and label the true grace gospel as "man-centered" or "man-centric" when in fact it is the lordship gospel that depends upon people getting themselves saved and keeping themselves saved through their own commitment, obedience, and sinlessness. Nobody is perfectly obedient or sinless in this lifetime. This clearly illustrates the problem with the lordship gospel and why it must be rejected, as its emphasis rests too greatly on people's ability to obey and commit/surrender. Their salvation message is dependent upon themselves. This makes their gospel no different than any other "works" religion.

As has been stated throughout this book, the Bible clearly communicates eternal security (purchased through the efficacious work of Christ) for those who simply put their faith in Christ and His work. Because Christ paid the penalty for sins, believers' sins never enter the equation in regard to their eternal destiny. They do, however, enter the equation for current fruitfulness/usefulness to the Lord on earth and for future heavenly reward (crowns). However, lordship advocates put too much emphasis on individuals and what they must do to stay saved or what they must do to prove that their salvation is genuine. Again, true biblical teaching tells one to "look away" to the Savior who bore his or her sins and not to look at oneself as a means of security — just like the bitten Israelites were to look away from themselves to the serpent on the pole in Moses' day.

The Second Superstructure Crack: Sanctification

Following the crack of eternal security, the second crack exposed with the lordship foundation is the believer's sanctification. Much like the topic of eternal security, both lordship and true grace teachers see sanctification as a biblical doctrine, and both even define the doctrine of sanctification the same! However, both sides recognize that they each still have glaring disagreements in the area of sanctification. For instance, the lordship position believes that the Bible guarantees a Christian *will* be progressively sanctified and *will* become progressively more holy as his or her life continues. In contrast, the true grace position holds that everything is in place (from a divine perspective) for the believer to grow progressively more holy in this life, but the believer must "live by faith" in God's provision to practically realize it. Because daily and moment-by-moment responses of faith are required from the believer, his or her sanctification cannot be guaranteed.

The lordship position does not teach that there are "carnal Christians." They unhesitatingly accuse true grace teachers of making the term up, and accuse them of being unbiblical. However, Paul himself used the term "carnal" when referring to Christians in 1 Corinthians 3, and the Corinthian believers were still even in that carnal state when Paul wrote them the letter.

Moreover, lordship teachers unbiblically say that it is impossible for the true believer to be dominated by sin in his or her life. The Bible does allow for the possibility that a true believer is dominated by sin in his or her life, but it in no way condones or promotes a believer to live this way. The difference between the lordship position and the biblical stance is the difference between the words "cannot" (lordship view) and "should not" (biblical view). It is shown biblically in Romans 6 that sin "can" still reign in the believer's life, but it "should not" reign in the believer's life.

Furthermore, regarding the doctrines of justification and sanctification, lordship teachers emphasize a direct link between justification and sanctification as they state that those who are justified **will be** sanctified (guaranteed). Therefore, according to them if one is not growing in holiness (being sanctified), then he or she was never truly justified. Lordship teachers focus on this area of progressive sanctification, as they like to visibly observe "holiness" in their own lives and others' lives. Hence, because their gospel is man-focused, their sanctification results in a man-centric focus.

In relation to the confusing arguments promoted by the lordship teachers, a couple of questions are posed. The first question is the following: If progressive/experiential sanctification is guaranteed (as lordship advocates teach), why do Christians not progress according to the same spiritual growth rate? The answer to this question, is that believers grow at different rates. This is seen in many biblical examples. The second question is as follows: If progressive/experiential sanctification is guaranteed, why do there appear to be different levels of reward at the judgment seat of Christ? The answer to this question, is that believers will be rewarded individually and at different levels at the judgment seat of Christ, indicating different and varying levels of fruitfulness. True biblical teaching tells people to look to or trust in God's provision for sanctification and not to look at themselves as a means of judging whether or not they are growing in holiness — much like the bitten Israelites with the serpent on the pole in Moses' day.

The Third Superstructure Crack: Legalism

Following the crack of a believer's sanctification, the third crack with the lordship foundation is the approach they teach for living the Christian life. Nobody wants to be called a legalist or wants to promote a legalistic approach to the Christian life. Legalism is defined (by both lordship proponents and free grace proponents) as using any law (man-made or God-given) to either gain justification and/or sanctification or to earn favor with God in general. Both free grace and lordship proponents describe legalism as dangerous for the Christian. However, because of lordship teachers' emphasis on commitment and surrender, their gospel can unfortunately lead to legalism in the Christian life. In fact, lordship teachers emphasize the Law's importance for the Christian in order to please God with his or her Christian life. Some lordship authors even question whether justification even ever took place in a believer who is not obeying the Lord's commands. Because of the Law's strict, perfect requirement it is odd that lordship teachers, in an effort to teach a self-sacrificing, commitment/surrender salvation, would allow for a lesser standard of compliance than what the Word of God teaches, but they do. They, in fact, do not require perfection as the Lord does! Lordship teachers soften the requirements by saying something akin to the following: "Well, if your heart desires to obey God, then your sincerity is good enough proof."

Lordship teachers teach the Law for the believer's life because they do not understand the Law's purpose given by Scripture. As discussed and reviewed in this book, the Law was given for the following reasons: (1) to establish a constitution of laws for the called out descendants of Abraham, known as the nation of Israel, (2) to stop every mouth — that is to muzzle every voice that would flaunt self-righteousness before God, (3) to produce in every human being a sense of personal guilt, accountability, and hence a need for God's forgiveness, (4) to provide an objective knowledge of sin for the human race, (5) to serve as a stern child disciplinarian to bring its hearers to Christ that they might be declared righteous by God through faith in Christ's finished work on the cross, and (6) to serve as a restrainer of evil and a perpetual <u>reminder to unbelievers</u> of their moral responsibility to God. The Law is categorically <u>not made for the believer</u>. In fact, nowhere in the Bible does the text say that one of the Law's purposes is for the believer to keep it in order to grow in holiness or Christlikeness.

Still, lordship teachers include the Law in the believer's life on the basis of the indwelling Holy Spirit. They teach that the indwelling Holy Spirit was given to enable the believer to keep the Law perfectly. However, this directly contradicts Paul's illustration of the marriage relationship in Romans 7. Through exegeting Romans 7, one sees that the believer's continued relationship with the Law is impossible from God's perspective, and, if the believer continues in that relationship, he or she will live an unfruitful life. God ended Christians' relationship to the Law by their death with Christ to it, and Christians have been married to another — the risen Lord Jesus Christ Himself — in order that they may bear fruit unto God. The very one who wrote and gave the Law (i.e. the Holy Spirit) is the very One indwelling

Christians. Hence, there is no need to focus or be occupied with a written external code in order to live a holy life, as when Christians depend upon the Holy Spirit, He produces the life of Christ in the believer. This life does not need to be subjected to the Law because the life of Christ is the Living Word of God and needs nothing external to curb or control His character. The believer is to look away from themselves for God's solution to be delivered from the power of sin in the Christian life.

Concluding Comments

Lordship salvation is the proverbial Christmas gift of coal, and, unfortunately, it is also the "gift that keeps on giving." Not only does lordship teaching impact one's justification message, but it also has lingering effects on one's sanctification message, including how one practically lives the Christian life. For this reason, the lordship gospel is more dangerous than one may think or realize. Not only does it keep unbelievers from enjoying the unhindered message of the good news of what Jesus Christ *did for people*, but it also causes Christians from all persuasions to live frustrated and fruitless Christian lives. In fact, the lordship message is one that deserves a like warning Paul shared in Galatians 1:8-9 which states, "But even if we, or an angel from heaven, preach any other gospel to you than what we have preached to you, let him be accursed. As we have said before, so now I say again, if anyone preaches any other gospel to you than what you have received, let him be accursed." The lordship gospel is a false gospel with far reaching effects — more than what is normally discussed. For this reason, it must be rejected and stood against in every way, shape, or form.

Scripture Index

OLD TESTAMENT

NEW TESTAMENT

ABOUT THE AUTHOR

Dr. John Thomas Clark holds his bachelor's degree in Mathematics from the University of Texas at San Antonio, has a master's degree in Theology (Th.M.) from Tyndale Theological Seminary and Biblical Institute, and his doctorate degree (DMin) with an emphasis on expository preaching from Dallas Theological Seminary. He values systematic, verse-by-verse Bible teaching and enjoys drawing out truths from the original languages. John has served as the Senior Pastor of Grace Community Fellowship in Newnan, Georgia since September 2016. Additionally, John is a founding board member of DM2 (Disciple Makers Multiplied), a mission organization focused on pastoral training and discipleship of other disciple-makers. John leads DM2's field to Liberia, Africa and travels there twice a year to train pastors. John's first and foremost ministry lies in being a husband to his wife, Carrie, and a loving father to their five children. For more teaching from Pastor John Clark, please visit www.gracenewnan.org